Room for Romance

FRANCE

The ultimate guide to romantic hotels

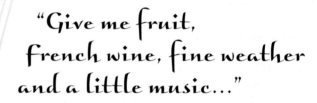

"Give me fruit,
french wine, fine weather
and a little music…"

John Keats

*f*alling in love with France is rather like falling off a log - it's impossible to resist. France seduces the senses, and the allure of this fabulous country is as strong as ever. In short - and as the French will tell you with a knowing smile - La Belle France is made for lovers. Go there not simply for wonderful food and wine, sublime countryside and a wealth of history, but for terrific places to stay.

Lovers love wonderful hotels, and you'll find the crème de la crème between these covers - whether you're heading to France for a fleeting weekend or a long, unhurried holiday. The 120 hand-picked properties that have made it into these pages range from the stylish and sybaritic to the intimate and bijou. If you and your grand amour are hankering after a sumptuous château in the Loire, a delectable auberge in Provence, a hedonistic hideaway in the Alps or a chic townhouse on the Rive Gauche, you'll find it here.

Some of our properties are decidedly au courant, others are grandly traditional, while yet more are true originals. Bed down in a troglodyte cave, slumber in canopied splendour in a château seemingly straight out of a Proustian novel, live like a prince and princess in the châtelain's own home, stay at a charming maison d'hôte that won't break the bank, or check into the plushest of palaces for the ultimate in indulgence.

While all the properties here are different in terms of style, location and price (and we say vive la différence!), we have picked them because they share not only a passion for great hospitality, but the flair, feel and philosophy that's tailor-made for a getaway à deux. Whichever places to stay you select - and we trust there will be many - we hope you'll love them as much as we do.

No matter whether you are falling for France for the first time, or whether you've had a long-standing love affair, you don't need an excuse to go. We hope the places to stay in **Room for Romance - France** inspire you to visit very soon.

Mairiona Cotter

FRANCE

Series editor	**Mairiona Cotter**
Editor	Mike North
Production and design editor	Claire Peters
Illustrations	Christine Coirault/frogillo.com
Maps	Joe Buckley
Website coordinator	Chris Shipton
Contributors	Sophie Mackenzie
	Melissa Shales
Research	Vicky Fox
	Ben Etherton
Hotel consultants	Dominic Hawkins (Paris)
	Maurice Moliver
	Michael Yeo
Publisher	Mairiona Cotter
Printing	Artes Gráficas Toledo
Distribution	Portfolio Books 020 8997 9000

Published in 2004
Freeway Media Ltd, 4 Ravey Street, London EC2A 4XX
T +44 (0)20 7739 1434   **F** +44 (0)20 7739 1424
info@room4romance.com   www.room4romance.com
info@freewaymedia.com   www.freewaymedia.com

ISBN 09-531746-6-2

While every care has been taken to ensure the accuracy of the information in this guide at the time of going to press, the publishers assume no responsibility for errors and omissions, nor for any loss, injury or inconvenience resulting from the use of information contained in this book.

Contents

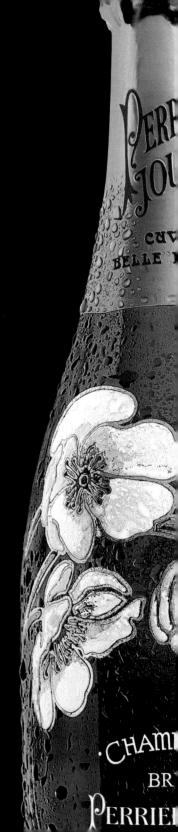

CHAMPAGNE PERRIER·JOUËT

Unforgettable.

Practicalities

What makes a Room for Romance?

All the properties in these pages have been chosen for their style, their standards and their romantic allure. Our choice of places to stay is not swayed by the stars and facilities which preoccupy other guides, but by the location, looks and loveliness of a property – a sense that its ambience and style make it tailor-made for romantic adventures. Each is unique, so whether your idea of romantic heaven is the swishest of châteaux or a rustic auberge dripping with charm (and we all have a different dream place) they are among the best of their kind.

Tariffs and taxes

The tariffs quoted on each page show the cost of a standard double room for two per night, and – where applicable – that of the best room or suite available. Rates are normally inclusive of TVA (France's equivalent of VAT) but not of local taxes. This so-called taxe de séjour (normally only a euro or two per person per night) varies according to the region, or département. Be aware that high and low season room rates can differ markedly, so do check when you are booking. Bear in mind, too, that some hotels may only accept two-night reservations at weekends.

While the prices quoted here were correct at the time of going to press, they can change without notice and inevitably creep up during the year. Take them as guidelines, therefore, rather than gospel. Do ask whether any special weekend or short break deals are available, since there are sometimes great savings to be made. Many Room for Romance hoteliers post details of their short breaks on our website, so do visit www.room4romance.com to check what's on offer.

Breakfast is priced separately and is normally continental style. Dinner prices should be taken as a guideline, since many hotels offer a range of prix-fixe menus at different prices, as well as a full à la carte menu – so depending on which you choose, your meal may cost a good deal more than the entry price shown.

Making an occasion of it

Do mention when you book if your visit is part of a honeymoon trip or other special occasion. Even if your chosen hotel does not offer a special celebration package as such, most will be delighted to arrange for champagne, chocolates or flowers to await you. Turn to page 160 for a list of some extras you may want to request.

Ne pas Déranger

Practicalities

Almost all the properties featured here accept payment by American Express and other major debit and credit cards. You will usually be expected to provide a card guarantee when booking, and cancellation fees may apply if you cancel at short notice.

Winter closures

Hotels in France tend to be more seasonal than in either Britain or North America, and winter closure (fermeture annuelle) is often the norm outside the cities and major tourist areas. Do check opening dates (shown on every page entry) before you book your flights, since some properties literally close their doors for three or four months during winter.

Dining in, and dining out

Francophile foodies can be assured of a great time in France. Dinner is rightly one of the big highlights of the day on a romantic getaway – and no-one understands that more than the French. La cuisine française is an art form, and the lure of gallic food and wine is the prime reason why so many bon vivants go to France year after year. Not, of course, that French cuisine needs to be haute to taste superb.

Some of the properties featured here have high-profile Michelin-starred chefs, while yet more have other impressive culinary accolades. Some have chic bars and bistros ideal for intimate suppers, while others are run by enthusiastic and dedicated couples who provide French regional cooking – cuisine du terroir – at its best. Proprietors who do not serve dinner in-house will be more than happy to suggest good places to dine where you'll enjoy anything from a no-holds-barred gastronomic feast to good, simple local dishes.

Although your idea of holidaying together may mean seeing as little of your fellow guests as possible, a few of the properties featured here offer guests the chance to dine together at a shared table often hosted by Monsieur or Madame. These dinners can be enjoyable and convivial affairs, so don't rule them out!

www.room4romance.com

Do visit our website at www.room4romance.com. You'll find a regularly updated bulletin board detailing news and seasonal offers, interactive maps and a picture of each property. You can also order further copies of this guide online, and email us your views and feedback. We award bouquets each year to the Room for Romance properties our readers tell us are the best, so we'd like to hear your views. Read more on pages 155 and 159.

Getting in touch

All our hotel entries show the international dialling code (+33) for France. Ignore the next (0) unless you are calling from within France. Mobile phone numbers usually start with (0)6.

Getting around

Roads in France are clearly graded. A roads (autoroutes) are toll-paying, while N roads (routes nationales) are free and generally carry less traffic. D roads (routes départementales) are minor country roads.

A basic glossary

A few words you may like to be sure of before setting off - and which crop up on many of these pages - describe the different types of accommodation offered in France, together with a few other useful items. Here's a handy list:

Auberge	Inn
Bastide	Old provençal country house
Café americain/allongé	Filter-style coffee - as opposed to strong black continental coffee (café) or milky coffee (café crème/café au lait)
Châtelain(e)	Lord (lady) of the manor
Chef-patron	Owner chef
Clos	Cloister
Cuisine du terroir	Regional cooking (produits du terroir: local produce)
Dégustation	Tasting - either at a wine cellar or in a 'tasting' menu
Demeure d'hôte	Upmarket Bed and Breakfast (otherwise: maison d'hôte)
Domaine	Estate
Eau gazeuze/plate	Sparkling/still water
Hostellerie	Hotel (in the old fashioned sense)
Hôtel de Ville	Not a hotel! This is the town hall
Lit à baldaquin	Four-poster or canopied bed
Logis	Lodge
Manoir	Manor house
Mas	Provençal farmhouse
Moulin	Mill
Ne pas déranger	Do not disturb
Potager	Kitchen garden
Relais	Inn
Service non compris	Service not included (also: service en sus)
Toile de Jouy	Fine French fabrics

Understanding the page entries

You'll find a sprinkling of French words and franglais throughout our pages. These are not italicised, since we reckoned that if (like us) you are fans of la vie française, you will probably have at least a smattering of French yourself. To save you from reaching for your phrasebook too often, here's how details on each property are arranged:

Bon repos	The bedrooms - what to expect in terms of style and comfort
Bon appetit	The food - both for breakfast and (where served) dinner
Bon temps	The diversions - things to do both in and around the property
Bon voyage	Getting there - from the nearest major town or city
C'est si bon!	What's special - and what we thought, in a nutshell

Similarly, on our map pages, you'll see:
Aller (great reasons to go); **Manger** (great local dishes); **Santé!** (great local drinks).

Symbols

The symbols shown with each entry denote facilities either at the hotel or nearby (normally within 10km). Do check first if a particular amenity is of special interest. The swimming symbol may denote a pool, or nearby beach swimming. The spa symbol may not denote a fully-fledged spa, and may signify that treatments like massage or aromatherapy are available, or that there is a sauna, solarium and fitness room. Again, we recommend that you check when booking. The disabled-friendly symbol denotes wheelchair access to at least one bedroom, as well as a hotel's public areas, while the smoking restrictions symbol can mean a ban in guest rooms, dining areas, or both.

Un très grand merci!

We are indebted to Dominic Hawkins, our Paris consultant, for working closely with us to help us identify the properties perfect for these pages. His knowledge, experience and translating expertise - and willingness to be contacted at all hours of the day - were an invaluable asset. Michael Yeo, our UK based consultant, also deserves special thanks.

Key to symbols

Note: swimming, tennis, golf and spa facilities may be on the property or nearby (usually within 10km).

Four-poster beds	Scenic setting	Spa facilities	Swimming	Tennis	Golfing	Weddings held	Disabled access	Smoking restrictions

france by region

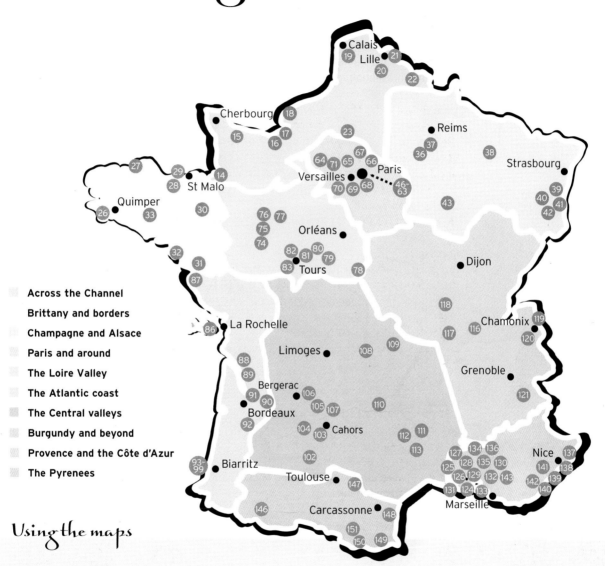

Calais
Lille
19
21
20
22
Cherbourg
18
Reims
17
23
37
15
16
36
38
Strasbourg
27
29
14
64
67
66
39
28
St Malo
71
65
Paris
40
41
26
Quimper
30
76
77
Versailles
70
69
68
46-63
42
33
75
Orléans
43
74
Dijon
82
80
79
118
Chamonix
119
31
83
79
Tours
78
117
116
120
87
Grenoble
86
La Rochelle
Limoges
108
109
88
121
89
Bergerac
106
110
91
90
105
107
Bordeaux
92
104
103
Cahors
112
111
127
134
136
Nice
93-99
102
113
125
128
135
130
141
137
Biarritz
126
129
132
143
142
138
Toulouse
147
131
124
133
140
139
146
Carcassonne
148
Marseille
151
150
149

Across the Channel

Brittany and borders

Champagne and Alsace

Paris and around

The Loire Valley

The Atlantic coast

The Central valleys

Burgundy and beyond

Provence and the Côte d'Azur

The Pyrenees

Using the maps

We have divided France into ten regions, each colour-coded for easy reference as shown. Each region has its own more detailed area map and introductory information. Hotel numbers refer to the page on which you will find the property's full details, and there are 120 in all. Our maps are not intended as navigation aids - make sure you take a proper road atlas if driving! - and are there primarily to show where hotels are located in relation to the nearest town, city or main road.

Across the Channel:
Normandy, Picardy and the North

Aller for le weekend
Manger delicious camembert, carbonnade flamande
Santé! Normandy cider, fiery Calvados, Flemish beer

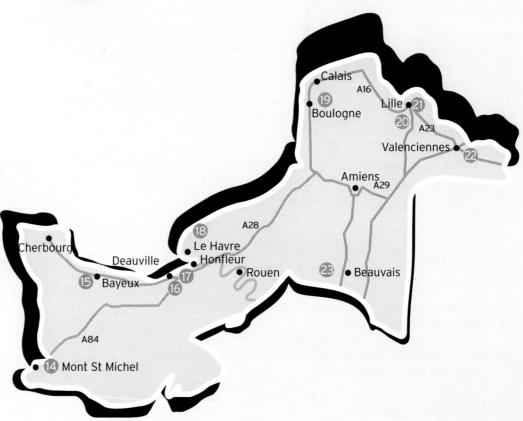

Rivers ———
Roads ———

Pages 14 – 23

Why?

Nowhere is more accessible than the swathe of northern France within an hour or two's drive of the Channel ports. It's both easy to reach and easy to fall for. From much-photographed Mont Saint Michel in the West to culture-packed Lille in the East, this region is packed with diverting things to see. Channel-hoppers can stock up on bargain booty in the hypermarkets of Calais and Boulogne on the way home.

So why not... ♥

- Watch artists at work in pretty Honfleur
- See the lilies in Monet's garden at Giverny
- Dip into the beaux-arts city of Lille
- Relive World War II history on Normandy's landing beaches
- Make time for le pique-nique – a fresh baguette, paté and some vin de pays never tasted so good!

Château de Boucéel

50240 Vergoncey
Tel: +33 (0) 2 33 48 34 61
Fax: +33 (0) 2 33 48 16 26
chateaudebouceel@wanadoo.fr
www.chateaudebouceel.com

Rooms and rates
2 rooms, 3 suites
Double room for 2 people
per night from €122 to €145
Breakfast included

Proprietors
Comte and Comtesse Régis de
Roquefeuil-Cahuzac

Open
All year round

Guests are welcomed as one of the family in this quite magnificent listed 18th century château. The family home of the Comte and Comtesse de Roquefeuil-Cahuzac simply oozes style and history. There's nothing stuffy about your hosts; they're gracious, relaxed and fun. Sumptuously appointed and panelled salons are decorated with innate good taste in Louis XV and XVI style. The grounds are no less distracting. Awaiting exploration are an English garden, a family chapel, a lake with swans and a stream crossed by a tiny lover's bridge. It's enough to go to one's head (but don't lose it, like the Comte's poor ancestors).

C'est si bon!

Aristocratic Normandy château where guests are indulged like family friends.

Bon repos Huge picture windows, lofty ceilings, family portraits, parquet floors, luxuriously draped beds with embroidered sheets... just the thing to encourage decadent languor. Alternatively, you could hole up in the rustic old Bakery, a pretty cottage in the grounds.

Bon appetit Breakfast is served in the elegant dining room with its comfortable high-backed chairs: look forward to home-made breads and croissants and farm-fresh delights. It's also delivered to your room (very noblesse oblige). Your hosts will recommend a host of good restaurants in the vicinity.

Bon temps Don't miss visiting the ancient Benedictine abbey of Mont Saint Michel, one of France's great sites (cross the sands by horse-drawn carriage when the tide is out). Be moved by the famous Normandy landing beaches, or hone your handicap on three nearby golf courses.

Bon voyage From Avranches-Mt. St Michel road take N175 at Exit 34; D40 for Antrain; D308 to St Senier de Beuvron.

Château de Goville

Départmentale 5
14330 Le Breuil-en-Bessin
Tel: +33 (0) 2 31 22 19 28
Fax: +33 (0) 2 31 22 68 74
chateaugoville@wanadoo.fr
www.chateaugoville.com

Rooms and rates
10 rooms 2 suites
Double room for 2 people
per night from €95 to €140
Breakfast €12. Dinner from €30

Director
Jean-Jacques Vallée

Open
All year round

Surrounded by 500 acres of parkland near the gates of ancient Bayeux, Château de Goville retains all the charm of a private home - albeit rather grander than most. Owner Jean-Jacques Vallée's family have lived here for nearly 200 years, and the house resonates with a sense of times past. Traditionalists will love the family portraits, chandeliers, richly painted walls and elegant furnishings, not to mention an awesome collection of antique dolls' houses in the gallery. Windows overlook a beautifully tended formal garden - styled à la française - beyond which stretches the luscious Norman countryside.

C'est si bon!

Echoes of a forgotten art de vivre here; heaven for nostalgia lovers.

Bon repos Individually themed bedrooms - each named after family members - have been decorated with care. One is a concerto in blues while another mixes pinks and off-white with deepest green. Prettily patterned bedspreads, softly draped curtains and rugs add warmth and welcome.

Bon appetit Breakfast comes complete with home-made rose or pear jams. Afternoon teas - a tradition here - are positively Proustian. Dinner is served in Le Carité restaurant, with its chequerboard marble floor and gilded mirrors. Diners have included cinematic grandes dames Lauren Bacall and Jeanne Moreau, so expect cooking to match.

Bon temps There's no need to leave the château for your fill of Norman history, says Monsieur Vallée - just listen to the walls talk. Outside, Bayeux and its famous tapestry await discovery. Push on to the coast, and the battles of World War II unfold at the D-Day landing beaches.

Bon voyage From Le Havre: take A29 then A13/N13 via Caen and Bayeux. Leave city ring road on D5 to Goville (exit 37.1).

Hostellerie de Tourgeville

Chemin de l'Orgueil
Tourgeville, 14800 Deauville
Tel: +33 (0) 2 31 14 48 68
Fax: +33 (0) 2 31 14 48 69
info@hostellerie-de-tourgeville.fr
www.hostellerie-de-tourgeville.fr

Rooms and rates
6 rooms, 19 apartments
Double room for 2 people
per night from €110 to €225
Breakfast €15. Dinner €38

Director
Wilhelm Stoppacher

Open
Except February

Built cloister-like around an enclosed quadrangle and set in 20 acres of parkland, this striking hostellerie was originally the 60's creation of famed film director, Claude Lelouche; a glamorous hangout for his celebrity friends. Nowadays you may not bump into a famous face every five minutes but its star quality hasn't dimmed. There's still pizazz. Traditional oak beams, flagged floors and country furniture are nicely counterpointed by modern pieces and materials, while pleasing colourways retain idiosyncratic touches. And as befits a top name in the movie business, there's also a private cinema. Ready for Take Two?

C'est si bon!

A class act - originally a clubhouse for stars of stage and screen.

Bon repos Rooms are decorated with relaxed chic. All benefit from private terraces and sun loungers, while the duplexes and triplexes with their separate floors feel more like apartments. Le Pavillon is an exquisite little manor house nearby - a tailor-made hideaway for two.

Bon appetit Rustically furnished dining areas have giant framed portraits of famous actors and actresses beaming down on diners. They must, however, share billing with chef Jean-Louis Farjot, whose menu of choice regional gastronomy makes him the leading man here.

Bon temps You're within easy reach of the coast, Deauville and Mont St Michel here. You could always stay inland exploring ancient cities like Caen (assuming you have energy left over from the hotel's pool and gym), stroll through the landscaped grounds or follow tranquil cycle routes through the Pays d'Aude.

Bon voyage From the A13 take the N177 towards Deauville. Join the D27 and turn left on to the D278.

Hôtel des Loges

18 rue Brûlée
14600 Honfleur
Tel: +33 (0) 2 31 89 38 26
Fax: +33 (0) 2 31 89 42 79
hoteldesloges@wanadoo.fr
www.hoteldesloges.com

Rooms and rates
14 rooms
Double room for 2 people
per night from €90 to €115
Breakfast €10

Proprietor
Catherine Chouridis

Open
All year round

When film maker Catherine Chouridis left the movie world she kept her keen eye for images and created a different kind of hotel in Honfleur, the scenic old Normandy fishing port. In converting three adjoining fishermen's houses she wanted a contrast to the traditional formula, so she's given full rein to her passion for contemporary interior design. The result is clean, uncluttered lines, chic simplicity and dazzling colour schemes. She has also opened a boutique opposite where guests can buy the very things they like about the hotel. Definitely one of the hippest addresses in fetching Honfleur.

C'est si bon!

Old fishermen's houses hiding snazzy interiors.

Bon repos Bedrooms look slick and modern with crisp soft furnishings. Each floor claims its own stylish colour scheme: plum and beige, russet and blue, grey and yellow. These follow through from walls to bed linen to carpeting. Expect sparkling baths and good lighting too.

Bon appetit There's a contemporary breakfast room with simple and charming crockery. Munch on crusty breads, home-made jams, local goat's cheese, farmhouse apple juice (have Calvados later!) and fresh fruits. It's also delivered to the rooms. Catherine advises on good local restaurants patronised by natives, not tourists.

Bon temps Spend time discovering the Normandy coast and sandy beaches - in particular this colourful fishing port with boats of all sizes crammed in the harbour (do go for a cruise). Visit the Satie and Boudin museums, galleries and antique shops, or meander into the countryside.

Bon voyage From Le Havre: take the N15 and D929 to Honfleur. Drop your bags at the hotel; parking 300m away.

Photos: R Malard

Le Domaine Saint Clair

Chemin St Clair
76790 Etretat
Tel: +33 (0) 2 35 27 08 23
Fax: +33 (0) 2 35 29 92 24
info@hoteletretat.com
www.ledonjon-etretat.fr

Rooms and rates
17 rooms, 4 suites
Double room for 2 people
per night from €90 to €300
Breakfast €14. Dinner from €35

General manager
Abo Dib

Open
All year round

Little wonder prominent figures of the fin-de-siècle arts scene gravitated to the circle of Camille de Saint-Phale, then owner of Domaine Saint Clair. This cliff-top enclave with handsome villa and ivy-clad Anglo-Norman keep framed by scented pines drew the likes of Proust, Monet, Flaubert and Offenbach. The ambience, and sweeping views of Etretat below, encouraged a rest from creative exertions and recharging of batteries. Their spirit remains, with palpable reminders of the Belle Epoque stretching across five salons whose decor doesn't lack theatrical impact. There's a pool and lovely terraced gardens, too.

C'est si bon!

Artistic hillside domain with an undeniably romantic vibe.

Bon repos You'll be torn between sleeping with Sarah Bernhardt in white-on-white serenity or with the glowing red and peach warmth of Camille. Named after famous figures, rooms are characteristically decorated (some with jacuzzis, private terraces and verandas). Each has views over sea, valley or gardens.

Bon appetit When it's warm, al fresco breakfast or lunch on the pool terrace is de rigueur. Indoors in the pretty mirrored dining room, chef and sommelier harmoniously work on menus dedicated to the five senses, with fine Normandy cuisine utilising flavours of the Med.

Bon temps Walk to the village, seashore, or along dramatic cliffs complete with world class golf course. Explore Normandy's countryside by car or horseback, alighting at 13th century Fécamp Abbey. Or pop into Le Havre for harbourside buzz, casino and Malraux museum.

Bon voyage Take the D925 from Dieppe, then D940, turning right before Etretat up a steep drive (marked).

Hôtel Cléry

Rue du Château
62360 Hesdin-l'Abbé
Tel: +33 (0) 3 21 83 19 83
Fax: +33 (0) 3 21 87 52 59
chateau-clery.hotel@najeti.com
www.hotelclery-hesdin-labbe.com

Rooms and rates
26 rooms
Double room for 2 people
per night from €57 to €155
Breakfast €11. Dinner from €25

General manager
Caroline Lefour

Open
All year round

What better place to stay as a first-nighter in France (you're just 12 miles from Boulogne and the Tunnel here) en route South, or as a base for a continental break just a short drive from the wine emporiums, cheese shops and hypermarkets of the Channel ports. Not that Hôtel Cléry should be regarded as a mere stepping-stone into France: its excellent restaurant, fresh decor and light-filled rooms make it a place worth settling into. Set at the end of a gated drive behind a billiard-board lawn in a peaceful five acre estate filled with trees and flowers, this pristine white-painted mansion makes a refreshing discovery.

C'est si bon!

Daisy-fresh overnight roost for Channel-hoppers.

Bon repos Shades of Laura Ashley here: attractive rooms – some in the main house, others in the cottages and farmhouse – are done out in florals, checks and pastels. Those on the top floor have gabled roofs and peaceful surrounds, overlooking graceful chestnut trees.

Bon appetit Dining in the light-filled, glass-walled restaurant is almost as good as being in the park itself. Wicker chairs and a terracotta stone tiled floor lend it a pleasingly summery feel, and the food's worth waiting for. Specialities include fillet of John Dory, crisp-coated and served with a Noilly Prat sauce.

Bon temps Pas de Calais has a wealth of footpaths and golf courses, not to mention a 12th century castle museum and the Nausicaa centre, highlighting life under the sea. If shopping is more your scene, take home a taste of France from Boulogne's many speciality stores and hypermarkets.

Bon voyage From Boulogne: take the N1 and join the A16 at Exit 28 (Isques-Samer).

La Howarderie

1 rue des Fusillés
59320 Emmerin
Tel: +33 (0) 3 20 10 31 00
Fax: +33 (0) 3 20 10 31 09
howarderie@nordnet.fr
www.lahowarderie.com

Rooms and rates
5 rooms, 3 suites
Double room for 2 people
per night from €135 to €155
Breakfast €15

Proprietor
Catherine Courcol

Open
Except Christmas - New Year

Lille's recent mantle as European City of Culture has made it a mecca for weekenders keen to tap into its rich seam of museums, stores and historic attractions. Few visitors realise, however, that you don't necessarily need to stay slap in the middle of the city to make the most of its charms. Ten minutes' drive from the centre of town is La Howarderie, a former 17th century Flemish farmhouse cocooned in rural peace, where you could be in another world. With its gables, spruce paintwork and pretty flowered courtyard, this is a place to trade urban buzz for rustic serenity.

C'est si bon!

A Lille touch of the country just miles from city bustle.

Bon repos Rooms are big on comfort and individually styled. The Adagio suite has its own deliciously private terrace – perfect for sunny, straight-out-of-bed breakfasts – while some have cosy beams, nicely fashioned furniture and antique wooden headboards. Faultless marble bathrooms have oversized tubs, while fresh flowers and fruit are a nice added touch. Staff know how to cosset guests, too.

Bon appetit Room service breakfast comes with silver crockery and linen napkins. Light dining treats such as foie gras with fig chutney can be rustled up later complete with choccies and champers. Book ahead, and your fizz will arrive with a gift of flutes engraved with your initials.

Bon temps This is great cycling terrain, and rural Flanders is on the doorstep. So too is Lille (pick-ups can be arranged), whose attractions now include an impressive collection of gardens from around the world, just a few miles away.

Bon voyage From Calais: take the A26 and leave at Exit 6 (N41) for Lille. Follow signs to Santes and Emmerin.

Hôtel Brueghel

3-5 parvis Saint-Maurice
59000 Lille
Tel: +33 (0) 3 20 06 06 69
Fax: +33 (0) 3 20 63 25 27
hotel.brueghel@wanadoo.fr
www.hotel-brueghel.com

Rooms and rates
65 rooms
Double room for 2 people
per night from €71 to €88
Breakfast €7.50

Proprietor
Danièle Lhermie

Open
All year round

Here's a charismatic little place bang in the middle of happening Lille. In fact it's down a quiet pedestrian street close to the rather magnificent Saint Maurice gothic cathedral. The hotel itself is a good-looking corner building in traditional Flemish brick. Owner Danièle Lhermie enthusiastically scours antique markets and has used her keen eye to decorate with idiosyncratic charm. Certainly the wrought-iron Edwardian lift with its concertina doors clanking open and shut adds merrily to the atmosphere. The hotel makes the perfect roost for a long weekend (easy with Eurostar) or stop-over on a French odyssey.

C'est si bon!

If you want a feel for Lille, this hotel's right at the hub.

Bon repos Rooms, individually decorated in harmonious colours, are intimately sized but don't feel cramped: each one is simply but charmingly furnished – many with interesting finds from local markets. Some have views towards the cathedral spires and cobbled square outside.

Bon appetit Wholesome continental breakfasts start the day; after that Danièle and her staff helpfully point guests towards the area's many trendy cafés and restaurants. Beers are truly flavoursome in this neck of the woods, so check out the local brews.

Bon temps As Northern France's capital, the city offers diversions both cultural and historic. Vieux Lille, with its gabled 17th and 18th century Flemish buildings, delights the eye, and there are plenty of chic stores to browse in. Lille also has lots of good museums, and the renovated old stock exchange with its florists, antiquarian booksellers and smart shops merits a visit.

Bon voyage hotel is 5-6 minutes' walk from TGV station.

Auberge du Bon Fermier

64 rue de Famars
59300 Valenciennes
Tel: +33 (0) 3 27 46 68 25
Fax: +33 (0) 3 27 33 75 01
beinethierry@hotmail.com
www.home-gastronomie.com

Rooms and rates
16 rooms
Double room for 2 people
per night from €119 to €126
Breakfast €9. Dinner from €24

Proprietor
Thierry Beine

Open
All year round

Sit yourselves down at a quiet table on the terrace in the Bon Fermier's cobbled courtyard: it echoed to the clatter of horses and carriages for nigh on five centuries. It's said that kings Henry IV and Louis XIV once stopped at this old staging post. Owner Thierry Beine has maintained the building's historic atmosphere, which oozes from a warren of welcoming nooks, crannies and little staircases. It's full of characterful bits and pieces: a suit of armour guards reception, for example. Window boxes burst with blooms; the town centre is right on the doorstep. Patron and staff graciously harness old-world charm to modern life.

C'est si bon!

Old 16th century coaching inn where you might get carried away.

Bon repos Monsieur Beine says guests sleep contentedly here (as they purportedly have done since the 1560's). Rooms are cosy: some come with beams and open brickwork, some are adorned with little tapestries, and all are furnished with pleasant provincial and rustic furniture. Bathrooms come with robes.

Bon appetit At night the restaurant is lit solely by candles, while Vivaldi plays in the background. Diners can tuck into creative regional cuisine (délicieuse!) cooked on a wood fuelled range. Options could include game, catch of the day or spit-roasted piglet. Snacks are served on the terrace.

Bon temps Arty? Two nearby museums feature Rubens, Wateau and Matisse. Sporty? There's riding, tennis and a couple of 18-hole golf courses. Weary? A health centre close by revives with aqua therapy. Ready to explore? Hop on a river cruise or potter around old towns and hamlets.

Bon voyage Take the A23, A2 or N30 to Valenciennes and follow signs to town centre.

Château de la Rapée

Bazincourt sur Epte
27140 Gisors
Tel: +33 (0) 2 32 55 11 61
Fax: +33 (0) 2 32 55 95 65
infos@hotel-la-rapee.com
www.hotel-la-rapee.com

Rooms and rates
12 rooms, 1 apartment
Double room for 2 people
per night from €81 to €110
Breakfast €11. Dinner from €31-41

Proprietors
Philippe and Pascal Bergeron

Open
Except February and 16 Aug - 9 Sept

Bedded in miles of deep forest, this 19th century Gothic mansion sits on a lofty plateau away from the world. Grand, steeply-roofed turrets, gables and ornate brickwork lend it a whimsical air, while indoors, all is cosiness and warmth. Touches of eccentricity abound: antlers and rugs enliven some of the downstairs walls, for instance. There's a real away-from-it-all tranquillity here, surrounded as you are by acres of woodland. Run for many years by the Bergerons - father and son - this is a place where cooking is taken seriously, and where only the sound of birdsong (or your beloved) should disturb your slumbers.

C'est si bon!

Grand setting for a Norman conquest?

Bon repos Play babes in the wood in individually styled bedrooms overlooking swathes of greenery. Some are quite stately, most are painted in creamy pastels, and all have the comforts you would expect.

Bon appetit Dining in the raftered, wood-panelled dining room, where a fire burns merrily on chill autumn nights, is a pleasure indeed. Chef Philippe Bergeron's menus make the most of Normandy's coastal bounties, with plenty of fresh scallops, trout, lobster and langoustines. Sweet-tooths are not ignored either, with crêpes au sabayon de cidre brut and tarte aux poire caramelisées among some yummy desserts.

Bon temps Laze by the pool on sunny days, play golf nearby or discover woodland trails and tranquil Normandy countryside. Gisors - capital of the Knights Templar - is close by, while Monet's house at Giverny is an easy ride.

Bon voyage From Dieppe: take the D915 towards Gisors. The hotel is 4km to the north, and signposted.

Brittany & borders:
The north-west and a bite of the Loire

Aller for fresh French leave
Manger coquilles Saint-Jacques, feather-light crêpes
Santé! Breton cider, crisp Muscadet

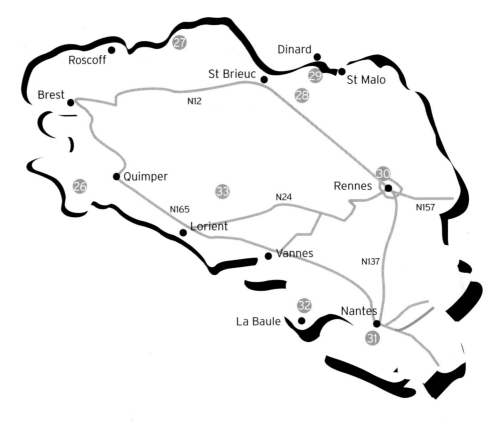

Rivers ——————
Roads ——————

Pages 26 – 33

Why?

Jutting out into the Atlantic, Brittany's rugged coastline has that breezy, good-to-be-alive fresh-air tang. This is the place for uncrowded beaches, rocky islets and watersports. Inland, you'll find sleepy towns and villages where you can step back in time among half-timbered houses and narrow streets. Tune into the Celtic vibe here – the Breton language still thrives, and locals love nothing better than to cock a snook at the rest of France.

So why not...

- Share some seafood on the rocks at pretty quayside cafés
- Wander around medieval Dinan and the walled city of Saint-Malo
- See the fabulous stone carvings of Les Rochers Sculptés at Rotheneuf
- Go and see the standing stones of Carnac
- Try your luck on the blackjack tables of Dinard's casino

Château du Guilguiffin

Le Guilguiffin
29710 Landudec
Tel: +33 (0) 2 98 91 52 11
Fax: +33 (0) 2 98 91 52 52
chateau@guilguiffin.com
www.guilguiffin.com

Rooms and rates
4 rooms, 2 suites
Double room for 2 people
per night from €130 to €150
Breakfast included

Proprietor
Philippe Davy

Open
All year round

Woods and a ravishing park surround this legendary 18th century château, which boasts nearly 1,000 years of history (get Monsieur Davy to share the tale of the 19th century Comte who, unable to face intimate relations with his less-than-alluring wife, threw her from a window, and was later forced to hand over the family silver in the divorce court). Today, this gloriously aristocratic château in wildest Brittany is a dream of a place, with richly gracious bedrooms, roaring fires, magnificent grounds and opulent furnishings. Plush with antiques, redolent with history and grand to its fingertips, it glows with times past.

C'est si bon!

History, great hosts and some of Brittany's loveliest gardens.

Bon repos Each of the rooms is individually styled. There's the yellow room, over the grand stairway, with its superlative view of the park; the blue room, whose bathroom is entirely decorated with hand-painted frescoes; or – for incurable romantics – the rose room, with its canopied king-size.

Bon appetit Staff serve breakfast in bed here, so you can stay cocooned till long into the morning. Order champagnes and aperitifs from the friendly bar staff, and indulge your appetite for great Breton shellfish at local restaurants.

Bon temps You might not discover original sin, but you could easily imagine yourself in the Garden of Eden here. Stroll along 11km of shady lanes, whose rhododendrons throw up a blaze of colour in early summer, and admire the geometric precision of the classical parterres. Further afield, riding and sailing will quench your yen for outdoor adventure.

Bon voyage From Quimper: take the D785 for Pont l'Abbé, then the D56 to the D784 towards Audierne.

Ti al Lannec

14 allée de Mezo-Guen
22560 Trébeurden
Tel: +33 (0) 2 96 15 01 01
Fax: +33 (0) 2 96 23 62 14
resa@tiallannec.com
www.tiallannec.com

Rooms and rates
33 rooms
Double room for 2 people
per night from €144 to €317
Breakfast €14. Dinner from €34

Proprietors
Danielle and Gérard Jouanny

Open
March – November

Back in the 70s Gérard and Danielle Jouanny discovered a neglected turn of the century house in Trébeurden, overlooking Brittany's sweeping coastline. Over the years they have renovated and rebuilt sympathetically, helping the place rediscover its soul. It's clearly been a labour of love. There's a mellow ambience here: large comfy sofas and fauteuils, chintz draperies, fresh flowers and huge stone hearths with blazing fires in winter. With its spruce and tiered verandas, the house enjoys terraced gardens bordered by pine and cypress trees. From its hilltop perch, a private path meanders down to beaches and coves below.

C'est si bon!

Splendid sea views and blissful balneotherapy.

Bon repos Wake up to sun streaming across the bed, then take breakfast on your own veranda with that bracing seascape all around you, or just sit and watch the waves on a moonlit night. If the weather turns chilly, cosy up in warm and individually decorated rooms.

Bon appetit Huge windows run alongside the dining rooms so nearly everyone gets a coastal view. Lights twinkle on the horizon at night, while candles glow close to. A choice of menus here includes plenty of Breton specialities – lots of seafood of course – cooked with flair.

Bon temps Enjoy the best of the coast by following heritage trails across cliffs and sands. The hotel's L'Espace Bleu Marine Spa indulges guests with cocooning body treatments, solarium, hydro-dynamic baths and jet showers. Outdoor lovers can try their hand at watersports, horse riding, billiards and golf.

Bon voyage From the N12, join the D767 for Lannion after Guingamp, then take D65 for Trébeurden.

Manoir du Vaumadeuc

22130 Pleven
Côtes d'Armor
Tel: +33 (0) 2 96 84 46 17
Fax: +33 (0) 2 96 84 40 16
manoir@vaumadeuc.com
www.vaumadeuc.com

Rooms and rates
11 rooms, 2 apartments
Double room for 2 people
per night from €90 to €190
Breakfast €10

Proprietors
Carol and Even O'Neill

Open
All year round on reservation

When Even O'Neill (yes, Irish roots here) took over his aunt's tired 15th century manor house he knocked it stylishly into shape. He and his wife Carol have created a warm and welcoming environment that's obvious the minute you cross the large flagstoned hall with its ancient oak beams, huge Tudor-esque fireplace, vases of flowers, mélange of comfortable antiques and soft glow from ironwork chandeliers. The place drips with atmosphere. A pretty Renaissance garden has a terrace scattered with tables to soak up the rustic tranquillity. Acres of parkland reach to the front door, enhancing the feeling of intimacy.

C'est si bon!

Medieval Breton manor offering calm, charm and blissful comforts.

Bon repos If you are not sliding beneath crisp sheets in the manor itself, you can bed down in one of the estate's two carriage houses. All are nicely appointed, and many have views. Room Four is intriguing: a wall-to-wall library runs right behind the bed, though we never discovered if it contained a copy of the Kama Sutra.

Bon appetit Light breakfasts are brought to bedsides, while more robust dishes are served in the pretty dining room. Dinner can be served by arrangement (especially when couples bring friends for an exclusive house party), and Even enjoys directing tastebuds to the area's many gourmet hotspots.

Bon temps Bracing walks through the forest of La Hunaudaye, on the doorstep, are easily juggled with trips to the beaches of the Côtes d'Armor ten minutes away. Go fishing, horseriding, play tennis or enjoy golf nearby.

Bon voyage From Dinard: take D768 to Plancoët, drive 2km towards Lamballe; take D28 towards Pleven. Manor on right.

Villa Reine Hortense

19 rue de la Malouine
35800 Dinard
Tel: +33 (0) 2 99 46 54 31
Fax: +33 (0) 2 99 88 15 88
reine.hortense@wanadoo.fr
www.villa-reine-hortense.com

Rooms and rates
7 rooms, 1 apartment
Double room for 2 people
per night from €130 to €205
Breakfast €13

Proprietors
Florence and Marc Benoist

Open
28 March - 5 October

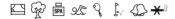

Young couple Marc and Florence Benoist run this handsome seafront villa, whose Belle Epoch flourishes remain intact. Built in the 1850s by Russian Prince Vlassov in tribute to Queen Hortense de Beauharnais, it's palatially inspired but intimately scaled. The interior, with period furniture and fin-de-siècle pieces, certainly looks inviting, and delicate floral stencilling on the panelling and main salon's ceiling is exquisite. Because of its aspect - looking across the bay to St. Malo - the large airy rooms capture all the glinting light of the sea. Dinard's famous beach is steps away below. The Benoists are charming, friendly and down to earth.

C'est si bon!

The sea's here but why not take a dip in Queen Hortense's silver bathtub.

Bon repos Rooms with balconies are perfect for sea-gazing - just clock those views! Interiors, with tall picture windows, are soothingly decorated and Empire beds generously sized. One ensuite boasts the regal silver bathtub of a Queen. Lie back and soak up the grandeur.

Bon appetit Good continental or English breakfasts are served in the small dining area, or brought to your room. Dinard doesn't want for fine cuisine: traditional Breton dishes capitalise on its reputation and location, with briny-fresh seafood and fish

Bon temps The Emerald Coast around Dinard, once a fishing village, now has smart holiday villas and old houses dotted among craggy cliffs, parks and gardens. Its counterpart, the genteel seaside resort of Saint Malo, has impressive ramparts. Both towns invite exploring.

Bon voyage From Paris: travel via Le Mans and Rennes on the A11 and N157. Signposted from the centre of town.

LeCoq-Gadby

156 rue d'Antrain
35700 Rennes
Tel: +33 (0) 2 99 38 05 55
Fax: +33 (0) 2 99 38 53 40
lecoq-gadby@wanadoo.fr
www.lecoq-gadby.com

Rooms and rates
11 rooms
Double room for 2 people
per night from €145 to €165
Breakfast from €18. Dinner from €40

Proprietor
Véronique Brégeon

Open
All year except 1 week in August

A distinctly Breton individualism colours the delightful LeCoq-Gadby, which in a city heavy with venerable associations is deemed to be something of an institution. This friendly maison bourgeoise opens onto a hidden orangerie, complete with clambering Queen Elizabeth roses. Inside elegantly furnished salons you'll find Celtic touches – plaids and tartans here and there – a billiard room and a bar Anglais where le scotch and le gin and tonic are generously measured. The sleek Armour Arcoat spa with its range of heavenly treatments and hammam soothes weary lovers.

C'est si bon!

Stylish spa promises rest and well-being, come Rennes or shine.

Bon repos Pretty rooms filled with antiques (some with balconies overlooking the rose bushes) follow two themes: Romantique – all swathes of delicate toile de Jouy cascading from bedheads – and Olympe, with echoes of classical Grecian draperies around four-posters.

Bon appetit Inventive fixed and à la carte menus reflect seriously good Breton cuisine featuring dishes from the region and excellent seafood and fish. We drooled over Caneton des Marais farci aux morilles et foie gras. There's a fine cellar, and gastronomic pleasures are heightened in the garden under sunny skies.

Bon temps You're at the heart of the ancient Breton capital of Rennes, so think half-timbered medieval buildings, ramparts, royal palaces and jousting grounds. There's also theThabor Botanical gardens, museums, markets and smart pedestrianised shopping.

Bon voyage From ring road, enter the city via Avenue Patton or Boulevard d'Armorique. Both join rue d'Antrain.

Abbaye de Villeneuve

44480 Les Sorinières
Tel: +33 (0) 2 40 04 40 25
Fax: +33 (0) 2 40 31 28 45
villeneuve@leshotelsparticuliers.com
www.abbayedevilleneuve.com

Rooms and rates
17 rooms, 3 suites
Double room for 2 people
per night from €80 to €190
Breakfast €13. Dinner from €24-€74

Proprietors
Les Hôtels Particuliers - Groupe Savry
Manager: Julien Vincendeau

Open
All year round

Peasants on the warpath in the late 18th century destroyed most of this 13th century Cistercian abbey founded by Constance de Bretagne, but there are still delightful left-overs. The large monumental staircase, flagged floors and cloisters, for example – though activity around them today is thankfully more pleasure than penance. And guests report that staying here is indeed a delight. The surroundings exude warmth, and there are plenty of comfortable armchairs and sofas to sink into. Floodlights on the building fore and aft at night make the scene even more beguiling.

C'est si bon!

Hotels like this former monks' habitat could well become a habit.

Bon repos Settle into an uncluttered nook whose spare but comforting elegance is offset by sturdy beams and stone walls; or pick a dramatic chamber painted cardinal red, with thick fabrics warmly draped. Neoclassical mosaics adorn some of the good-size bathrooms.

Bon appetit Starched white table linens, gleaming glass and silverware, candlesticks and a huge fireplace set the tone in L'Epicurien, which occupies the original part of the old cloisters. Diners will enjoy religiously tucking into a choice of classical and regional dishes.

Bon temps A striking circular pool provides the focus in good weather, while fine Atlantic beaches beckon not far away. Sporting stuff nearby includes golf, riding, fishing and tennis. Make time to take a gander at Nantes with its flower-filled botanical gardens, Gothic architecture and museums.

Bon voyage From Nantes: take the A83 south, turning off at Exit 1 (La Roche sur Yon). Take the D178 for Viais.

Castel Marie-Louise

1 avenue Andrieu, BP 409
44504 La Baule
Tel: +33 (0) 2 40 11 48 38
Fax: +33 (0) 2 40 11 48 35
marielouise@relaischateaux.com
www.castel-marie-louise.com

Rooms and rates
29 rooms, 2 suites
Double room for 2 people
per night from €153 to €525
Breakfast €18. Dinner from €55

General manager
Arnaud Bamvens

Open
Except 15 November - 15 December

This handsome turn of the century Breton country house overlooks a terrace which overlooks a sweep of landscaped garden which in turn overlooks La Baule, one of the country's best beaches. What it doesn't overlook is comfort, immediately apparent from the welcome and the art de vivre which follows through in the mix of well chosen neo-classical, rustic and 1930s antiques, chandeliers and tapestries. Guests start feeling pretty languid reclining on one of the lawn's sunloungers – perhaps following an al fresco breakfast gazing down to the sea, pine trees gently swaying in the Atlantic breeze. Mmm, la vie est belle.

C'est si bon!

A Belle Epoque manor house fronting one of France's finest beaches.

Bon repos Patterned fabrics, wallpapers and soft furnishings are coordinated or contrasted to create cosy antique-filled havens. Some rooms might hold a four-poster, while in others you'll find generously swathed bedheads. If the Breton sea air doesn't induce sweet dreams, there's 24-hour room service.

Bon appetit Chef Eric Mignard has a reputation for creativity: he draws on his Lyon roots and experience gained in leading kitchens to create unpretentious haute cuisine from seafood, farm-fresh produce, and locally reared poultry. There's a strong wine list, too.

Bon temps Explore the bay's magnificent sandy beaches on foot or horseback. Enjoy tennis, watersports, thalassotherapy, three golf courses (including the 45-hole Barrière La Baule). Engage with the countryside too and discover the Guérande salt marshes. There's a casino and nightclub nearby, so you can bet on a good time.

Bon voyage Enter La Baule from N171 and follow signs.

Château du Launay

Launay
56160 Ploërdut
Tel: +33 (0) 2 97 39 46 32
Fax: +33 (0) 2 97 39 46 31
info@chateaudulaunay.com
www.chateaudulaunay.com

Rooms and rates
10 rooms
Double room for 2 people
per night from €125 to €180
Breakfast €10. Dinner €20

Proprietor
Christophe Bogrand

Open
Except January - Easter

The hosts at this sophisticated Breton château promise a taste of medieval romance – and we don't think they mean chastity belts! Whether you're enjoying a musical evening in the drawing room, a foray into the surrounding woods on horseback, or some R&R in your elegantly appointed suite, you'll feel as if you've stepped back in time to a seductively leisurely age. The house is surrounded by 150 hectares of forest, fields and a small lake, and set in the heart of the Morbihan region. This is the country of ancient druids, so who knows what magic charms linger here still. Anyone for love potion?

C'est si bon!

Grand living, and a pool that's wired for sound: float to heavenly music.

Bon repos Huge, graciously appointed and bathed in sunlight – the rooms here are elegance itself. Wooden floors, fireplaces, canopied beds and rich colonial touches are matched by roomy bathrooms, contemporary art pieces and sweeping views over the surrounding parkland. Squires and damsels never had it so good.

Bon appetit Breakfast from the banquet-style buffet table here is generous and fresh. And no problem if you'd sooner not get up – say the word and it will be brought to you in bed. Dinners here are convivial; join your fellow guests around the huge polished oak table.

Bon temps Bait your hook and see what catch today will reel in, stroll in the forest, curl up with a book in the leather-chaired library, or challenge each other to a love-match at billiards. Riding and tennis are also on offer, while the gym and hammam await.

Bon voyage From St Malo: take the N137/N12/N164 to Pontivy, then the D782/D1 to Toubahado. Turn right; signed.

Champagne & Alsace:
Bubbly country and the eastern borders

Aller for a grape escape
Manger tarte flambée and spaetzle - local noodles
Santé! fragrant rieslings or champagne - what else!

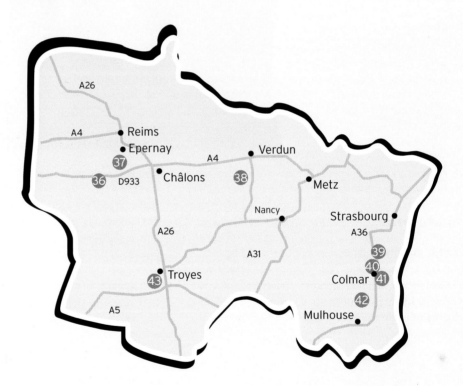

Roads ————

Pages 36 – 43

Why?

Champagne bubbles with history – not to mention France's most famous tipple. Come here for fabulous fizz, visits to the famous cellars of Reims and Epernay and some gastronomic good living. Alsace is a colourful contrast, with shades of Bavaria in its half-timbered Hansel 'n' Gretel villages. Vine-covered hillsides blaze with gold in autumn.

So why not...♥

- Visit the grand old champagne houses of Epernay and Reims
- Gaze at magnificent Reims Cathedral, a survivor of two world wars
- Pick a local menu champenois to accompany your bubbly
- Follow the fabled route du vin through pretty Alsace wine villages
- Drift through the canals of historic Colmar by boat

Château d'Etoges

4 rue Richebourg
51270 Etoges
Tel: +33 (0) 3 26 59 30 08
Fax: +33 (0) 3 26 59 35 57
contact@etoges.com
www.etoges.com

Rooms and rates
20 rooms
Double room for 2 people
per night from €110 to €190
Breakfast €12. Dinner from €30

Proprietor
Anne Filliette-Neuville

Open
Except 25 January - 12 February

Cross the moat to the grounds of this graceful 17th century château, and you'll find yourself surrounded by the charm and atmosphere of olden days. Rooms are decorated with antiques and tapestries, and the 18 acres of park encircling the château are studded with ornamental fountains, ponds and statues. A favourite stopover for travellers en route from Paris to Strasbourg, it has played host to many of the kings of France as well as to the court of Emperor Napoleon. Home to the same family for 150 years, this grandly moated château promises the warmest of welcomes in what remains very much a family home.

C'est si bon!

Could be the place where Napoleon said 'Not tonight, Joséphine...'

Bon repos The 20 high-ceilinged bedrooms are decorated in opulent French style: think floral soft furnishings, richly patterned wallpaper, Louis XVI chairs and delicately painted wood panelling. Beds, of course, are pure Liaisons Dangereuses.

Bon appetit The elegant, chandeliered dining room is the setting for to-die-for dinners. Goose roasted in honey, foie gras cooked with brandy, lobster with saffron and baby vegetables are just a few of the tempters on offer. A glass or two of the local champers makes the ideal prelude.

Bon temps In this neck of the woods, there's surely no better way to spend a day than visiting local champagne caves, and, as Dom Perignon so memorably put it, 'drinking the stars'. If the stars go to your head and a little R&R is called for, cycling, punting, billiards, or just a quiet afternoon in your suite are all on offer...

Bon voyage From Paris: exit A4 at Ferté sous Jouarre. Join the D407/D933 and follow signs to Châlons-en-Champagne.

Royal Champagne

51160 Champillon
Epernay, Marne
Tel: +33 (0) 3 26 52 87 11
Fax: +33 (0) 3 26 52 89 69
royalchampagne@relaischateaux.com
www.relaischateaux.com/royalchampagne

Rooms and rates
20 rooms, 5 suites
Double room for 2 people
per night from €270 to €300
Breakfast from €20. Dinner from €55

General manager
Andrea Ricci

Open
All year round

This former 18th century coaching inn, ivy clinging to neat white brickwork, was where Emperor Napoleon and his entourage rested en route to Reims. Back then the interior was comfortable but more simple: today it's invitingly luxurious. Nothing faux here either. Exquisitely furnished in a proper French version of country house, it feels soft and harmonious. Staff are obliging. What's more, the hotel's position overlooking the Marne Valley is a stunner: lush slopes dotted with old villages and vineyard after vineyard stretch away into the distance. And the champagne town of Epernay is just down the road.

C'est si bon!

Napoleon loved staying here for the champers, and so will you. (We don't know about Josephine).

Bon repos Each of the 25 rooms – opt for the newer courtyard rooms for a swish contemporary feel – has its own terrace with views over the valley. Sit outside with a glass of Buck's fizz and drink in the view with your morning croissants. Note that bathtubs have glass rests. Cute, non?

Bon appetit The Royal Champagne restaurant has a Michelin star, so expect to dine a treat from four menus embracing the best of cuisine française. The cellars boast some 300 vintages of champagne and fine wine. Don't be overawed; the sommelier is helpful, not haughty.

Bon temps Get a fresh perspective of vinous countryside by helicopter; accompany local growers around their domains; take cellar tours and tastings. Cruise along the River Marne to Reims, impressive cathedral city where France's kings were traditionally crowned.

Bon voyage Take the A4 from Paris, joining the N3 to Epernay near Château-Thierry. Take the N2051 towards Champillon at Epernay.

Château des Monthairons

55320 Dieue sur Meuse
Tel: +33 (0) 3 29 87 78 55
Fax: +33 (0) 3 29 87 73 49
accueil@chateaudesmonthairons.fr
www.chateaudesmonthairons.fr

Rooms and rates
20 rooms
Double room for 2 people
per night from €70 to €155
Breakfast €12.50. Dinner from €32

Proprietors
The Thouvenin family

Open
Except 1 January - 7 February

This fairytale castle, complete with turrets, chandeliers, sweeping staircases and sumptuous cuisine, offers a taste of what living happily ever after is all about. Its 35 acres of parkland sweep down towards the River Meuse, where a private beach awaits. Romanesque and Gothic chapels invite exploration and quiet contemplation, and nature lovers can check out the birds at the heron centre. The Meuse river valley is Joan of Arc country, and the area is also home to many moving and sobering reminders of World War I, so it's steeped in all-too-human history – ideal, then, for lovers both indolent and intellectual.

C'est si bon!

The stuff story books are made of – Cinderella never had it so good!

Bon repos The château's 20 rooms include four spacious duplexes with cosy private lounges downstairs. The first-floor rooms are chic to a degree, with high ceilings and freestanding bathtubs in the bedroom.

Bon appetit This place is gourmet heaven – the chef takes his craft seriously, so choose between classy à la carte and tasting menus. Expect to feast on foie gras, lobster, escargots, trout, pigeon and more. Sea bass is cooked on a bed of salt; a lavender infusion scents the veal; and only the olive oil is virgin. Had your fill? Then it's time to head upstairs, murmuring, 'Please, sir, can I have some amour?'

Bon temps Visit nearby Verdun, world capital for peace and a fascinating historic centre with its battle scars and relics of the Great War. The countryside is tailor-made for two-wheeled travel, or if you prefer, simply lounging by the river or strolling hand in hand through the château's park.

Bon voyage From Paris: take the A4 and leave at Verdun exit. Follow signs to Ancemont and D34 to Monthairons.

Le Clos Saint-Vincent

Route de Bergheim
68150 Ribeauvillé
Tel: +33 (0) 3 89 73 67 65
Fax: +33 (0) 3 89 73 32 20
clovincent@aol.com
www.chateauxhotels.com/saintvincent

Rooms and rates
20 rooms, 4 suites
Double room for 2 people
per night from €97 to €215
Breakfast €14. Dinner from €33

Proprietors
Arthur and Emmanuel Chapotin

Open
Mid March - mid November

Tucked between the trees in a scenic corner of Alsace, this pleasingly intimate inn surveys a sweep of rolling vineyards stretching away to the Black Forest and the Alps just a stone's throw from the German and Swiss borders. Snuggled in the valley below are the spires and half-timbered houses of Ribeauvillé, one of the region's picture-perfect wine villages. There's little to disturb the peace here, and the hotel's relaxing air makes it a great place to unwind. Views are omnipresent, whether you're drying off by the pool, dining in the first-floor restaurant or on the canopied terrace, or relaxing on your top-floor balcony.

C'est si bon!

Everything's tickety-boo and tranquil here in the heart of Alsace wine country.

Bon repos Guestrooms are comfortably done out with rugs, mellow wood furniture and pleasing fabrics. Most are designed to make the most of the views, with full-length French windows and a balcony where you can soak up the evening sun.

Bon appetit Fingers crossed for fine weather here: dining out on the terrace is an unmissable treat, with a vista of vineyards and hills unfolding into the distance, and a bottle of one of the cellar's crisp rieslings ready to uncork. House specialities include calves liver cooked in pinot noir.

Bon temps This is a great base for exploring Alsace's aptly named route du vin - especially during September's wine festival season. Visit vineyards and caves, the Haut-Köenigsbourg castle and the car museum at Mulhouse - the biggest of its kind. Relax in the hotel's indoor pool or stretch out on a chaise longue after your day's endeavours.

Bon voyage From Strasbourg: take the A35 to Colmar, turning off after Sélestat on the D106 for Ribeauvillé.

La Maison des Têtes

19 rue des Têtes
68000 Colmar
Tel: +33 (0) 3 89 24 43 43
Fax: +33 (0) 3 89 24 58 34
info@la-maison-des-tetes.com
www.la-maison-des-tetes.com

Rooms and rates
21 rooms
Double room for 2 people
per night from €91 to €235
Breakfast €13.50. Dinner from €29.80

Proprietors
Carmen and Marc Rohfritsch

Open
All year round

The intricate stone facade of this impressive Renaissance building in the heart of historic Colmar excels itself with its 105 gargoyles, and is listed as a historic monument. Behind its striking exterior is a delightful high-sided and balconied courtyard where tables are at the ready on warm days. Owners Marc and Carmen Rohfritsch have enthusiastically restored the hotel's previously worn-out interior by pepping up the best bits of its Alsatian heritage. Guests staying here have the best of Colmar - a centuries-old cathedral town with bags of charm and great shops - on their doorstep.

C'est si bon!

Atmospheric building of the Middle Ages with ageless appeal.

Bon repos Colourful motifs painted by a local artist adorn the guest room doors, beyond which you'll find generously sized beds, simple but elegant furnishings and nicely modern bathrooms, some with jacuzzis. All rooms are air-conditioned, and those tucked up high into the eaves, with views across the rooftops, will appeal to lovebirds.

Bon appetit Heavily panelled dining rooms are criss-crossed by ancient beams supporting period chandeliers and hung with intricate Eggemann frescoes over which light reflects from leaded windows. Gourmet menus and fine Alsace vintages are rightly to be savoured in the Maison des Têtes restaurant.

Bon temps Among Colmar's cultural highlights are the Musée Auguste Bartholdi (his great sculptures include the Statue of Liberty) and Musée Unterlinden, whose superb altar piece rates as one of France's great art treasures.

Bon voyage Take the A35 and N83 from Strasbourg, then follow signs to city centre.

Hostellerie le Maréchal

4-6 place six Montagnes Noires
68000 Colmar
Tel: +33 (0) 3 89 41 60 32
Fax: +33 (0) 3 89 24 59 40
marechal@calixo.net
www.hotel-le-marechal.com

Rooms and rates
30 rooms, 2 apartments
Double room for 2 people
per night from €95 to €245
Breakfast €12.50. Dinner from €35

Proprietor
Roland Bomo

Open
All year around

Some places look almost too good to be true, and Le Maréchal - looking like a make-believe gingerbread house about to topple into a pool of runny honey - is one. In reality it's a solid half-timbered 16th century building securely tucked beside a canal in Colmar's much-photographed Little Venice quarter. Inside the property original beams can be seen everywhere, butting against delicately stencilled surfaces. Giant candelabra and generous flower displays nudge prettily painted walls strewn with plates and pictures. The result is ravishing. Manager Alexandre Bomo adds a convivial warmth.

C'est si bon!

Looks like a Hansel and Gretel fairytale house; works like magic on guests.

Bon repos Rooms are all beamed ceilings and pretty hues. Four-poster and canopied beds are swathed in lush brocades, while decor and period furniture exemplify the smarter Louis styles. Nothing old about the bathrooms, though: many boast whirlpools and power showers.

Bon appetit On warm evenings romance beckons at candlelit terrace tables by the canal. The mood inside the more formal L'Echevin, with its classical background music, is deliciously enticing too. How does ballottine of Alsatian squab with duck liver and truffles sound?

Bon temps Colmar's water-encircled old town is a gem. Come fine weather, taking a bateau along the canal is a must for views of the original 11th century ramparts. Hot-foot around the town's ancient closely-packed streets to take in its museums and timbered facades, or drive out to vine-clad countryside.

Bon voyage Take the A35 and N83 from Strasbourg. When entering Colmar, follow signs to Petite Venise.

hostellerie Saint-Barnabé

68530 Murbach-Buhl
Alsace
Tel: +33 (0) 3 89 62 14 14
Fax: +33 (0) 3 89 62 14 15
info@hostellerie-st-barnabe.com
www.hostellerie-st-barnabe.com

Rooms and rates
27 rooms
Double room for 2 people
per night from €76 to €183
Breakfast €14. Dinner from €28-80

Proprietors
Clémence and Eric Orban

Open
Mid Feb - late Dec (not 24-26 Dec)

Built in hospitable Alsatian style, this 100-year-old hotel exudes a friendly, almost jolly air. Stripey awnings, flower-decked verandas, shutters and stencilled doors set the tone. Located on the old Roman Way, it's snugly set within pretty grounds surrounded by the firs and ferns of the Vosges hills. Young owners Eric and Clémence Orban are charm itself, too, making the place feel homely yet sophisticated. He is an accomplished chef, while Madame capably sees to the running of the house. The couple stress Saint Barnabé's other great virtues: rustic peace and tranquillity.

C'est si bon!

Triple pleasures here: French most definitely, but with Swiss and German accents too.

Bon repos Rooms are large and individually decorated in crisp bright colours. Some have balconies offering restful forest views. There's also a cosy chalet in the grounds whose log cabin atmosphere makes a nice nest for those planning a lovefest.

Bon appetit An oak-beamed dining room with vast marble hearth and armorial embellishments sets the scene. Today's knights and damsels will melt over succulent dishes like pigeon d'Alsace in gingerbread butter served with acacia honey and cider-flavoured onions. Spiffy Alsatian wines to match.

Bon temps This part of France almost converges with Germany and Switzerland, so long walks, bike rides and exploratory drives through pretty countryside are de rigueur. Visit Murbach Abbey nearby; go skiing in season; play mini golf in the grounds or visit famous vineyards.

Bon voyage Take the A35 from Strasbourg, then the N83 south. Take D430 past Guebwiller to Buhl and Murbach.

La Maison de Rhodes

18 rue Linard Gonthier
10000 Troyes
Tel: +33 (0) 3 25 43 11 11
Fax: +33 (0) 3 25 43 10 43
message@maisonderhodes.com
www.maisonderhodes.com

Rooms and rates
7 rooms, 4 suites
Double room for 2 people
per night from €98 to €168
Breakfast €15

Proprietor
Thierry Carcassin

Open
All year round

The Gothic spires and splendour of medieval Troyes await outside the doors of this renovated 16th century mansion, once owned by the Templars and now transformed into an architecturally dazzling place to stay. Beyond its heavily timbered frontage (whose appeal is anything but wooden), interiors are a ravishing mix of the old and contemporary. Minimalism mixes with splashes of lavish: rough stone walls and bold wooden beams are counterpointed with ornate mirrors, fireplaces, state-of-the-art bathtubs and sleek wooden furniture. Beyond the cobbled courtyard, the narrow streets and gabled roofs of Troyes await.

C'est si bon!

Bags of panache in the old capital of Champagne.

Bon repos Individuality is the order of the day (and night) here. Bold design flourishes lend rooms both a rustic and urban loft feel: gigantic beds dressed in sumptuous white linen are set on terracotta floors, while bathtubs are designed to make indulgent soaking a double act.

Bon appetit Al fresco breakfasts in the hotel's medieval garden will set you up for further gastronomic guzzling around town. Champagne is definitely the tipple here (Troyes was the former capital of Champagne, remember), and many eateries offer taster glasses. Santé.

Bon temps You're in the heart of town here, just yards from the Cathedral St-Pierre-et-St-Paul, the Museum of Modern Art, and streets lined with half-timbered houses. Beyond the old city walls, it's a case of grape expectations: the vineyards and rolling countryside of Champagne stretch away.

Bon voyage From Paris: leave on the N19 then take the A5 to Troyes. Follow signs to city centre.

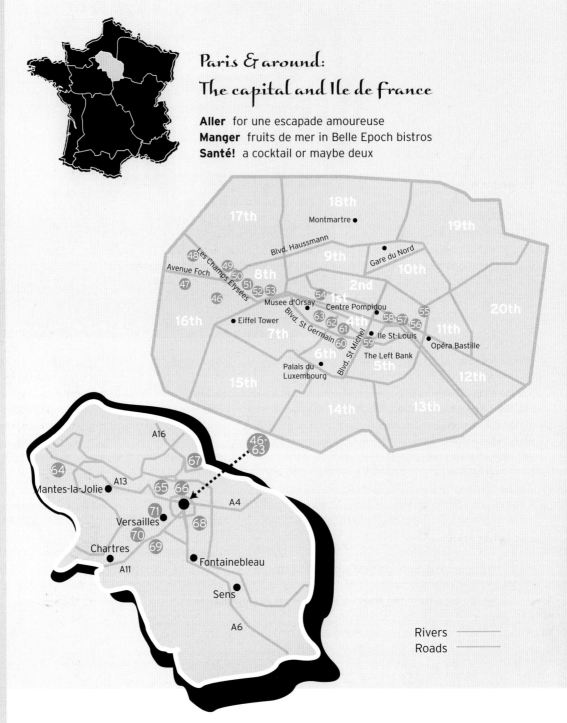

Paris & around:
The capital and Ile de France

Aller for une escapade amoureuse
Manger fruits de mer in Belle Epoch bistros
Santé! a cocktail or maybe deux

17th
18th
Montmartre ●
19th
Blvd. Haussmann
9th
Gare du Nord
10th
Les Champs Elysées
48
49
50
8th
2nd
20th
Avenue Foch
47
51
52 53
54
1st
46
Musee d'Orsay
Centre Pompidou
55
16th
● Eiffel Tower
Blvd. St Germain
63
62 61
4th
58 57 56
11th
7th
60
59
Ile St-Louis
Opéra Bastille
6th
The Left Bank
Blvd. St Michel
5th
15th
Palais du
Luxembourg
14th
13th
12th

A16
46-63
67
64
A13
65 66
Mantes-la-Jolie ●
A4
71
Versailles ●
68
70
Chartres ●
69
A11
● Fontainebleau
Sens ●
A6

Rivers ——
Roads ——

Pages 46 – 71

Why?

Paris is the quintessential city for lovers. This metropolis of lovely boulevards, brasseries and bridges makes it capital for romance. Shop in bijou stores in the up-and-come Marais; join café society in Saint Germain; stroll down the monumental Champs Elysées; mooch in the galleries of the Left Bank; enjoy le weekend Parisien visiting world-class museums.

So why not...♥

- Stroll hand-in-hand through the Bois de Boulogne
- Browse the bric à brac shops of Place des Vosges
- Soak up the view from the steps of Sacré Couer in Montmartre
- Splash out on expensive silk lingerie
- Watch the bâteau-mouches from the banks of Ile Saint Louis

Trokadéro Dokhans

117 rue Lauriston
75116 Paris
Tel: +33 (0) 1 53 65 66 99
Fax: +33 (0) 1 53 65 66 88
reservation@dokhans.com
www.dokhans.com

Rooms and rates
45 rooms
Double room for 2 people
per night from €400
Breakfast €26

General manager
Marie-Louise Corsius

Open
All year round

The Left Bank may have plenty of bohemian buzz, but for those who would rather stay on the Right, Dokhans is the chic place to be. In the heart of the classy 16th arrondissement (think smart brasseries and well-heeled stores), this wedge-shaped fin-de-siècle building has been styled throughout by top French designer Frédéric Mechiche. As well as trawling Paris antique markets for unusual decorative pieces he has mixed the classic and contemporary with huge flair. Neoclassical detailing contrasts with modern art and antique wood panelling to beguiling effect. Plenty of Wow factor here.

C'est si bon!

Hip hangout in the 16th, complete with champagne bar.

Bon repos Choose from statement-making rooms with contrasting moods. One attic suite is done out entirely in Ming blue while another is black and white with splashes of gleaming wood. The duplex Eiffel suite offers a great view of the famous tower. Elegant furniture, statuary and velvety curtains are mixed with panache.

Bon appetit The hotel's seductively wood panelled champagne bar is the setting for breakfast (what better excuse to start the day with a glass of bubbly!). It reverts to bar mode in the evening – with a different house champers each week – when there's also light dining. A tea room caters for mid-afternoon hunger pangs.

Bon temps You're within walking distance of the Arc de Triomphe and the Eiffel Tower (climb it after dark for the best views), not to mention the Art Deco Trocadéro itself. The area is also tailor-made for strolling, with its quiet streets, grand residences and smart shops.

Bon voyage Nearest metro: Trocadéro. Also valet parking.

Saint James Paris

43 avenue Bugeaud
75116 Paris
Tel: +33 (0) 1 44 05 81 81
Fax: +33 (0) 1 44 05 81 82
contact@saint-james-paris.com
www.saint-james-paris.com

Rooms and rates
48 rooms
Double room for 2 people
per night from €345 to €480
Breakfast €20-25. Dinner from €55

General manager
Tim Goddard

Open
All year round

If London's Pall Mall personifies that exclusive little world of gentleman's clubs then its spirit is superbly replicated in the Saint James, though thankfully without the stuffiness. This handsome neoclassical château is the business: acres of impressive marble, panelling and pillars, sweeping staircase, galleried reception rooms, and dozens of leather armchairs to sink into. What could be an overtly clubby and masculine interior has been artfully softened by an elegance that's appealing to both sexes. There is a well equipped health club and pleasing garden. The hotel also functions as a private members club; certainly worth joining.

C'est si bon!

Paris's only château hotel with an unusually large garden - another plus.

Bon repos Individually decorated rooms come with smart contemporary details. They're large and quiet too, offering fountain or garden views. The ten rooms and suites on the top floor boast their own intriguing glass-covered private terraces. Bathrooms are well appointed, with many having double basins.

Bon appetit The panelled dining room has doors opening onto a gorgeous terrace for fine weather dining. And this is fine dining - period. Chef Cyrille Roberts' classical menu changes daily according to market conditions: just try the heavenly poached foie gras with liquorice. The library bar hosts jazz on Fridays (weekends start here!).

Bon temps The Saint James lies in the fashionable west (near the Arc de Triomphe) so just head east for all those famous landmarks. Alternatively, unwind or get worked up in the splendid health club, stroll around that garden, or ensconce yourself in the library with one of 12,000 titles.

Bon voyage Nearest metro: Porte Dauphine.

Hôtel Pergolèse

3 rue Pergolèse
75116 Paris
Tel: +33 (0) 1 53 64 04 04
Fax: +33 (0) 1 53 64 04 40
hotel@pergolese.com
www.hotelpergolese.com

Rooms and rates
40 rooms
Double room for 2 people
per night from €195 to €350
Breakfast from €12-19

Proprietor
Édith Vidalenc

Open
All year round

Modernism needn't mean minimalism with clinical cool passing as fashion. The Pergolèse proves it. Behind its 19th century facade lies some exciting contemporary living. A warm palette of colours complements clean lines of blond wood, while a curvy glass wall runs alongside the dark and intimate bar, letting light flood in from an inner courtyard. Custom-designed leather armchairs and specially woven rugs grace polished parquet floors. Walls are hung with paintings by Hilton McConnico and furnishings bear the signature of designer Rena Dumas. Colours may make bold statements but the place definitely has soul.

C'est si bon!

Where the French metropolis happily meets up with the funky and modern.

Bon repos Half the rooms are street side, the other half have views over the courtyard. Some may be small but all are light, airy and fresh. Bathroom surfaces shine in steel, glass, marble and chrome. There are three snug little attic rooms and the top-floor Chambre Pergolèse – drenched in sunlight and strewn with cushions – is a peachy dream.

Bon appetit The dining room is decorated in perky primaries, an uplifting start for a good buffet breakfast. (A continental breakfast can also be delivered to your bedside along with videos and DVD players, encouraging long lie-ins). Light meals are also served.

Bon temps Proximity to the Arc de Triomphe is the first stepping stone to the city's great sights, but why not check out alternatives? For example, the fashionable Marais, new-wave boutiques and eateries; the fast-changing bar and club scene; what's hot, what's not. Obliging young staff are happy to point the way.

Bon voyage Metro: Charles de Gaulle Etoile or Argentine.

Hôtel de Banville

166 boulevard Berthier
75017 Paris
Tel: +33 (0) 1 42 67 70 16
Fax: +33 (0) 1 44 40 42 77
hotelbanville@wanadoo.fr
www.hotelbanville.fr

Rooms and rates
37 rooms, 1 suite
Double room for 2 people
per night from €165 to €200
Breakfast from €13

Proprietor
Marianne Moreau

Open
All year round

Here's a place with the Eiffel Tower just within its sights that feels more like a private home than a hotel. Minutes from the Arc de Triomphe, family-run Hôtel de Banville combines splashes of 1930s charm with interiors blending the classic and contemporary. Inside, it's all resolutely top of the range stuff following a top-to-bottom renovation: plump sofas, mellow woods, soft lamps, extravagant drapes, and old oil paintings. There's a piano and fireplace in the salon (and a piano bar on Tuesday nights), an oversize silver ice bucket where chilled champers awaits – and staff who know the art of making you feel chez vous.

C'est si bon!

Plum address well worth making tracks for.

Bon repos Tranquil, airy bedrooms (with free broadband access for net addicts) range from sunny to intimate. Some have dreamy creams, gentle pastels and frothy canopies; others sport elegant striped wallpapers, deep wood furniture and smart prints. Bathrooms are worth wallowing in, with deep, clawfoot baths for lovers, side-by-side basins and expensive chrome fittings.

Bon appetit Start the day with a generous buffet-style petit déjeuner. Choose La Chambre d'Amélie, with its private balcony, and you could be breakfasting gazing over Paris rooftops to the Tour Eiffel. Staff are happy to suggest good dining spots in the vicinity.

Bon temps You're not far from the action, and a short metro ride takes you to the capital's blockbuster sights, museums and Latin quarter. Head in the other direction and you can bargain-hunt in the flea markets or admire the giant arch of La Défense.

Bon voyage Nearest metro: Porte de Champerret.

Hôtel Vernet

25 rue Vernet
75008 Paris
Tel: +33 (0) 1 44 31 98 00
Fax: +33 (0) 1 44 31 85 69
reservations@hotelvernet.com
www.hotelvernet.com

Rooms and rates
42 rooms, 9 suites
Double room for 2 people
per night from €280 to €550
Breakfast from €27. Dinner from €55

General manager
Alexander Scarvelis

Open
All year round

You'll find the Vernet down a small street running parallel with the Champs Elysées, close to the Arc de Triomphe. Rooms are all decorated with refinement and restraint, but don't make the mistake of thinking this equals dull. Au contraire: it has something of a buzz. There's the stylish and intimate bar for a start, and an illuminated glass-domed restaurant designed by Champigneulle and Eiffel (yes, the very same) whose magnificence takes your breath away; not to mention a hedonistic spa at the nearby Royal Monceau. The staff philosophy is that clients are 'for spoiling, not just room numbers.' It works.

C'est si bon!

Trad address with trendy lounge bar, domed restaurant and feel-good spa.

Bon repos Think comfort, comfort, comfort. Well appointed rooms reflect quiet good taste, with restful colour schemes, heavy draped curtains, quilted beds with fine linens, good lighting and striking flower arrangements. Lavish marble bathrooms come with jacuzzis, Bulgari products, kimonos and slippers.

Bon appetit Diners can enjoy Eric Briffard's gastronomy – described as 'passionate, full-bodied and sensual' (who are we to argue?) beneath the arched glass dome of Les Elysées. Trained under Joël Robuchon, his cooking emphasises seasonal flavours and authenticity. Cocktails in the exotic Jaipur Bar are all the Raj with trendy Parisians.

Bon temps The Vernet is bang in the middle of Le Triangle d'Or, which means easy access to the city's golden sights and chic shopping. The concierge's gold keys will help unlock access to tout Paris, and there's golden relaxation in the Royal Monceau's Thermal Spa.

Bon voyage Nearest metro: George V.

Hôtel Napoléon

40 avenue de Friedland
75008 Paris
Tel: +33 (0) 1 56 68 43 21
Fax: +33 (0) 1 47 66 82 33
napoleon@hotelnapoleonparis.com
www.hotelnapoleonparis.com

Rooms and rates
102 rooms, 12 apartments
Double room for 2 people
per night from €320 to €680
Breakfast €22. Dinner from €40

General manager
Ludovic Corpechot

Open
All year round

If you fancy somewhere worldly, plush, with room service 1,440 minutes a day and a concierge on call, the Napoléon fits the bill. Inspired by the Emperor himself and immortalised in Jean Gabin movies, this well located Paris landmark is a carefree skip from the Arc de Triomphe. It has recently undergone swanky renovation: many of the public salons are decorated with Napoleonic motifs, and graced by Empire and Directoire furnishings. Ceilings with chandeliers and frescoes glow under filtered light. It looks, and feels, smart and glossy. Stars stay here from time to time: the late Errol Flynn loved it.

C'est si bon!

Actor and roué Errol Flynn affectionately called it 'The Place'.

Bon repos Rooms are supremely comfortable; those with their own terrace feel close enough to touch the Arc de Triomphe (well, almost), while others have views across rooftops to the Tour Eiffel. Bathrooms are heavily topped and tailed in marble, with bathrobes for lolling in.

Bon appetit Get a kick from the Napoléon house cocktails in the Bivouac Café Lounge Bar's clubby confines (with wood fire in winter) before sampling some of chef Olivier Legentil's delectable Med-based lunch dishes or dinners. Take advantage of the pavement terrace in good weather, and soak up some streetlife.

Bon temps Paris is eminently walkable, and the hotel's enviable position means you can easily cover the city's top sights on foot. So, for example, it's a mere five minutes for retail therapy on Rue du Faubourg Saint Honoré, 15 to Les Halles and the Pompidou Centre and 20 to the Louvre. Need we add, there's masses in between day and night.

Bon voyage Metro station: Charles de Gaulle.

Hôtel de Vigny

9-11 rue Balzac
75008 Paris
Tel: +33 (0) 1 42 99 80 80
Fax: +33 (0) 1 42 99 80 40
reservation@hoteldevigny.com
www.hoteldevigny.com

Rooms and rates
26 rooms, 11 suites
Double room for 2 people
per night from €395 to €725
Breakfast from €21. Dinner from €59

General manager
Charles Bourdin

Open
All year round

One of the capital's best-kept secrets, Hôtel de Vigny is pure luxury. Done out with stroke-me fabrics in sunset shades highlighted by the odd flash of purest white, this elegantly plush townhouse cocoons you in comfort. Log fires in winter, warm wood panelling and temptingly filled bookshelves create the atmosphere of a supremely comfortable private home. The hotel's name pays homage to the great French romantic poet Alfred de Vigny, and perhaps his legacy will inspire you to pen a few love sonnets of your own... if you're not too busy flexing your credit card on the nearby Champs Elysées, that is.

C'est si bon!

And so to bed... beneath the glass-domed ceiling of one of the stunning suites.

Bon repos Individually decorated by Nina Campbell, bedrooms drip with Parisian chic. You'll find nothing less than Bulgari lotions and potions laid on in the marble bathrooms, some of which have jacuzzis. Velvety towels and bathrobes come as standard.

Bon appetit The low-lit Art Deco style Baretto bar and restaurant makes an inviting setting for dinner, and serves traditional French cuisine as well as more international dishes. The carte des vins is an impressively weighty affair. If the lure of your suite proves too strong, you can stay in and order room service 24 hours a day.

Bon temps With the Champs Elysées and the Arc de Triomphe on your doorstep - not to mention the rest of monumental Paris - there's no excuse for not getting out and exploring. Ask the concierge about tickets to the Moulin Rouge, treatments at the Villa Thalgo spa, and other indulgent treats.

Bon voyage Metro: George V or Charles de Gaulle Etoile.

Hôtel Lancaster

7 rue de Berri, Champs Elysées
75008 Paris
Tel: +33 (0) 1 40 76 40 76
Fax: +33 (0) 1 40 76 40 00
reservations@hotel-lancaster.fr
www.hotel-lancaster.fr

Rooms and rates
49 rooms, 11 suites
Double room for 2 people
per night from €470 to €590
Breakfast from €28. Dinner €70

General manager
Régis Lecendreux

Open
All year round

The Lancaster glistens like a secret gem just off the glitzy Champs-Elysées. This small ancien régime haven with five exquisitely decorated salons and serene honeysuckle scented courtyard is simultaneously both grand yet understated. Pastel coloured damasks, silks and linens, specially woven carpets and fine Louis XVI furniture are counterpointed by select contemporary pieces. The mood it engenders is classic, soft and glowing. Owner Grace Leo-Andrieu has injected her own inimitable style here (and won numerous awards), while staff follow her dictum that attention to detail and exemplary service mean everything.

C'est si bon!

No sugar-candy glitz here - this is the epitome of restrained glamour.

Bon repos Lovers' dilemma: so choose between the smouldering lilacs of the Marlene Dietrich suite (the Diva once lived here); the golden opulence of the Emile Wolf suite (the hotel's founder); or the secluded intimacy of Suite 80, which occupies the entire eighth floor. Bathrooms are sleek and ultra modern.

Bon appetit The café-bar has recently been upgraded to restaurant status, as conceived by three Michelin-star chef Michel Troisgros of Roanne fame. This is cooking of the highest order, a modern take on French classics. In summer, dining extends into the leafy courtyard.

Bon temps The location could hardly be bettered; you're a minute's walk from the Arc de Triomphe and the bars and bistros of Paris's best-known boulevard. You might happily spend the day just people watching, but swanky haute couture boutiques and some serious shopping beckon.

Bon voyage Nearest metro: George V or Franklin Roosevelt.

Opéra Richepanse

14 rue du Chevalier de Saint-
George, 75001 Paris
Tel: +33 (0) 1 42 60 36 00
Fax: +33 (0) 1 42 60 13 03
richepanseotel@wanadoo.fr
www.concorde-paris-hotel.com

Rooms and rates
35 rooms, 3 suites
Double room/suite for 2 people
per night from €230 to €590
Breakfast from €14

Proprietor
Edith Vidalenc

Open
All year round

It's all cool Art Deco here, with elegant 1930s furniture, mirrors and marquetry. Design purists will love the spot-on attention to detail – even the mouldings in the foyer were custom-made to fit the period style – and the look is clean and well-heeled. Rich blues and creams with splashes of dark suede and artfully sculpted flowers lend an air of restrained 30s glam. Staff are just as civilised, and the best of Paris is on your doorstep: the hotel is just a stone's throw from museums, monuments and wide tree-lined boulevards. You won't be chalking up many taxi or metro fares here.

C'est si bon!

Chic address with plenty of big-city buzz.

Bon repos Rooms – some with beamed ceilings and boldly patterned bedspreads – offer oodles of space and are thoughtfully kitted out with everything from towel warmers to make-up mirrors. Suites are more like fully-fledged apartments, with original art, a living room and twin-basin bathrooms.

Bon appetit Tuck into a generous breakfast buffet in the cheerful stone-vaulted dining room or – if you're splashing out – on the balcony of the spacious Madeleine suite, with its vista of Paris rooftops. Restaurants in abundance for a dinner à deux are minutes from the front door.

Bon temps It's almost a case of embarras de richesse here: where to start? Soak up vintage Paris on the doorstep – you're minutes from the Opéra, the Louvre and the Champs Elysées. Indulge in a lovers' tiff in the Jardin des Tuileries, then make up in style by window-shopping for a rock at one the glitzy jewellers of Place Vendôme.

Bon voyage Nearest metro: Madeleine or Concorde.

Pavillon de la Reine

28 place des Vosges
75003 Paris
Tel: +33 (0) 1 40 29 19 19
Fax: +33 (0) 1 40 29 19 20
contact@pavillon-de-la-reine.com
www.pavillon-de-la-reine.com

Rooms and rates
56 rooms
Double room for 2 people
per night from €335 to €410
Breakfast €20-25

General manager
Yves Monnin

Open
All year round

Place des Vosges in the Marais has drifted in and out of fashion since it was first constructed in the 17th century and frequented by Molière and Racine. The area's now achingly cool again and the smart Pavillon fits in neatly. Ivy clad and hiding behind a flowered courtyard, it observes the owner's dictum that it should feel as welcoming as her own home (memo to self; redecorate!) The decor artfully combines rustic and urban sophistication; fabrics and colours complement and contrast winningly. Panelling and beams decorate walls and ceilings; rugs cover flagstones; an imposing chimneypiece hosts log fires.

C'est si bon!

Chic mansion tucked behind the Marais' loveliest square.

Bon repos Deluxe, superior, duplexes, two-bed suites... each is individual but all are unified by stylish details – whether beamed, co-ordinated with stripes, checks or toile de Jouy. Some rooms are four-poster; beds are wide and bouncy. Soak up such comforts with drinks from the honesty bar.

Bon appetit Guests breakfast beneath the whitewashed vaults of a cellar decorated with tapestries. Baguettes and flaky-fresh croissants are delivered by the bakery right next door. In French hands, simple food when well done as here, is a veritable feast.

Bon temps The Marais buzzes. You can get a kick simply walking through the arcades and antique shops of Place des Vosges, and exploring nearby galleries, boutiques and cafés. Nearby is the historic Jewish quarter, museums dedicated to Picasso and Rodin, fabulous shopping and the Place de la Bastille.

Bon voyage Nearest metro: Bastille or St Paul.

Hôtel Lutèce

65 rue Saint-Louis-en-l'île
75004 Paris
Tel: +33 (0) 1 43 26 23 52
Fax: +33 (0) 1 43 29 60 25
hotel.lutece@free.fr
www.hoteldelutece.com

Rooms and rates
23 rooms
Double room for 2 people
per night from €130 to €180
Breakfast €10

Director
Roland Buffat

Open
All year round

Completely renovated in 2000, this is one of a quartet of Paris hotels owned by Roland Buffat. Sitting pretty in the heart of Ile Saint-Louis – a blissful little oasis with the Seine flowing past – it's the kind of place that lets you pretend, just for a few days, that you're a real Parisian. Built on six floors (with a lift), the lobby is filled with antique chairs grouped around an open fireplace, leading to a tranquil little courtyard filled with extravagant plants. The bar – richly decorated in wood and fabrics – offers inviting corners in which to write postcards home or pen the odd billet-doux.

C'est si bon!

A touch of Vieux Paris in the heart of Saint-Louis.

Bon repos Rooms are small, as in most of Paris, but the tiled bathrooms are bigger than most, beds are bouncy and the colours soft and serene. Some have beams, and Room 662 has a view over the Paris rooftops worthy of La Bohème.

Bon appetit Continental-style coffee and croissants are served in the brick barrel-vaulted cellar. For lunch, buy a picnic at one of the local delis and take it down to the quay, where you can sit beneath the poplar trees with Notre Dame in your sights. Staff will help you pick out a cosy eaterie for the evening, complete with candles, checked tablecloths and outdoor summer terrace.

Bon temps You couldn't be better placed for exploring Paris. Notre Dame, the Louvre and the Musée d'Orsay are within easy strolling distance, while the quay for boarding the glass-roofed bateau-mouches that ply up and down the Seine is just down the street.

Bon voyage Nearest metro: Pont Marie or Cité.

Hôtel des Deux Iles

59 rue Saint-Louis-en-l'ile
75004 Paris
Tel: +33 (0) 1 43 26 13 35
Fax: +33 (0) 1 43 29 60 25
hotel@2iles.com
www.2iles.com

Rooms and rates
17 rooms
Double room for 2 people
per night from €140 to €158
Breakfast €10

Director
Roland Buffat

Open
All year round

Ever since Abélard and Héloïse's ill-fated love affair nearly 800 years ago, Ile Saint Louis has been a place of bucolic picnics and hidden liaisons. These days it's no different; an oasis of quiet charm at the heart of a city of romance. Hôtel des Deux Iles fits neatly into the setting, a 17th century mansion converted with style into a welcoming home away from home, its baroque plasterwork and wood panelling sitting comfortably alongside antique furniture and lush flowers. The Ile itself is crammed with restaurants, cafés, creperies and delis, not to mention Berthillon, home of the finest icecream in Paris (look for the queue).

C'est si bon!

The perfect place to get
a feel for the Ile.

Bon repos Compact bedrooms, some with beams, are simply but prettily done out using provençal blues, yellows and reds, fabric walls and bamboo. The bed takes up most of the space (are we complaining?), but then that's Paris too!

Bon appetit Breakfast is in the barrel-vaulted cellar, warmed by a roaring log fire in winter. Friendly staff are happy to suggest a cosy bistro or two for the evening, and you can always stroll the streets for inspiration.

Bon temps Put on your walking shoes – Paris is at your feet, from the Ile de la Cité, with the domes of magnificent Notre Dame, to the heavily scented flower market in Place Louis Lépine. Cross to the Left Bank for the Quartier Latin, home of student Paris, while on the Right Bank, royal Paris stretches before you, with the Louvre, the Palais Royale and the Jardins des Tuileries. For something more contemporary, try the incomparable art collections of the Musée d'Orsay and the Centre George Pompidou.

Bon voyage Nearest metro: Pont Marie or Cité.

Caron de Beaumarchais

12 rue Vieille du Temple
75004 Paris
Tel: +33 (0) 1 42 72 34 12
Fax: +33 (0) 1 42 72 34 63
hotel@carondebeaumarchais.com
www.carondebeaumarchais.com

Rooms and rates
19 rooms
Double room for 2 people
per night from €120 to €152
Breakfast €9.80

Proprietors
Alain and Etienne Bigeard

Open
All year round

Caron de Beaumarchais, who wrote the *Marriage of Figaro*, actually lived a few doors up from the hotel named after him in the fashionable Marais. But Etienne and Alain Bigeard, father and son, pay homage with striking fidelity. In the main salon there's a rare 1792 pianoforte (of the type Mozart used to create his gorgeous score); an antique backgammon table; plenty of 18th century memorabilia and ephemera, and soft background music (no prizes for guessing whose). The decor has been charmingly rendered in a fresh and light French Gustavian style mixing period pieces. There is also a little secret garden.

C'est si bon!

Tune into this little treat, inspired by the writer of *Le Mariage de Figaro*.

Bon repos Susannah and Figaro, the comic opera's protagonists, endure various discomfitures before finding wedded bliss. Guests are spared such hurly-burly: intimate spaces are restfully appointed in a style that marries Nordic calm with French chic (soundproofed too – should you be contemplating a highly decibelled duet).

Bon appetit If you'd sooner lie in and turn petit déjeuner into brunch, they do it here with some style. It's served until midday in the breakfast room, and you can enjoy it from your balcony perch in fine weather. Up for lunch? Trust the Bigeards' local recommendations.

Bon temps There's plenty to sing about, as this little lot are all within easy walking distance: the Opéra Bastille, Place des Vosges, Ile Saint-Louis, the Louvre, Notre Dame, the Pompidou Centre and the Carnavelet Museum. Some guests are not surprisingly happy enough simply hanging out in the Marais.

Bon voyage Nearest metro: Hôtel-de-Ville.

Les Rives de Notre Dame

15 quai Saint-Michel
75005 Paris
Tel: +33 (0) 1 43 54 81 16
Fax: +33 (0) 1 43 26 27 09
hotel@rivesdenotredame.com
www.rivesdenotredame.com

Rooms and rates
10 rooms
Double room for 2 people
per night from €130 to €290
Breakfast €11

Proprietors
Danièle Limbert and Christian Martin

Open
All year round

Step inside this small ten-roomed hotel in the heart of the Latin Quarter and you'd think for all the world you were in Provence or Tuscany. Behind its 16th century facade, rooms radiate the warmth and atmosphere of both places: think tiled floors, ochre-painted walls and exposed brickwork, beams, lush ferns, flowers and delicate fretwork furniture. The sitting room has an attractive domed glass and beamed ceiling beneath which guests can enjoy drinks and gaze up at the stars. The staff are as sunny as the environment they have created. And the bustle of Notre Dame is just a few steps away, naturellement.

C'est si bon!

A cute little place in Paris that cleverly conjures up Provence.

Bon repos Soundproofed rooms are individually decorated in colours evoking the South of France; we're talking duck-egg blues, canary yellows, soft vanillas and burnt orange. Soft furnishings in breezy checks and ginghams underline the mood, while attractive bathrooms have terracotta floors and marble-topped basins.

Bon appetit Tasty petit déjeuners, continental or buffet style, are served in a primrose-coloured dining room whose zinginess won't fail to enliven morning sleepy-heads. And good times (not to mention late nights) are assured in the many good local restaurants.

Bon temps The hotel is ideally located along the quay on the Left Bank, with views towards Notre Dame cathedral. On one side there's Rue Saint Jacques, on the other the famous Boulevard Saint Michel; and all around the buzz of cafés, galleries and chic boutiques that's Saint Germain. So... make like a boulevardier?

Bon voyage Nearest metro: Saint-Michel.

Odéon Hôtel

3 rue de l'Odéon
75006 Paris
Tel: +33 (0) 1 43 25 90 67
Fax: +33 (0) 1 43 25 55 98
odeon@odeonhotel.fr
www.odeon-hotel.com

Rooms and rates
33 rooms
Double room for 2 people
per night from €170 to €270
Breakfast €10

Director
Véronique Fraenkel

Open
All year round

Rue de l'Odéon, where this historic listed 18th century mansion with cobbled courtyard sits, is rich in literary associations. French writers such as Valéry, Gide and Claudel fraternised at Number seven, while Joyce, Eliot and Hemingway congregated at Number 12. Here's a case for bedding down at Number three: it's contemporarily decorated in reds and creams, making it feel warm and relaxed, even funky. It also feels calm. Couples without any literary pretensions could well find the atmosphere in the bar, with a glass of champagne perhaps, inspires them to scribble sweet nothings.

C'est si bon!

Parisian charm and
oomph in Saint Germain.

Bon repos What's your fancy? Choose from dramatic papal red walls and ancient beams; or surfaces and ceiling covered in a bold blue and green plaid (strangely soothing); or warm apricot cosiness. Whatever, each room radiates individual style and comfort. Modern bathrooms enjoy Roger & Gallet toiletries.

Bon appetit Stay snug in your room for continental breakfast, served till midday. You'll get the works: fresh juices, breads and jams, steaming beverages, cereals, cheeses and yoghurts. Should see you through to dinner.

Bon temps The Odéon sits at the crossroads of several worlds, all easily walkable. On the doorstep, there's Saint Germain itself - heaving with chic street life; the Quartier Latin around the Sorbonne, all book stores, intellectual buzz and student bars; the Luxembourg Gardens, a relaxing and flowery green space with tennis; and bistros, bars and brasseries galore.

Bon voyage Nearest metro: Odéon or Saint-Michel.

Hôtel d'Aubusson

33 rue Dauphine
75006 Paris
Tel: +33 (0) 1 43 29 43 43
Fax: +33 (0) 1 43 29 12 62
reservationmichael@hoteldaubusson.com
www.hoteldaubusson.com

Rooms and rates
50 rooms
Double room for 2 people
per night from €260 to €410
Breakfast €23

Proprietor
Pascal Gimel

Open
All year round

Lovebirds celebrating a special occasion couldn't do much better than bed down in the d'Aubusson. This splendidly renovated 17th century mansion in the heart of Saint Germain gives cupid's endeavours a bit of va va voom with a pre-bookable romantic VIP package. Goodies include limousine pick-ups, champagne lunch laid on in your room, red roses, tickets to concerts and cruises plus specially arranged dinners and shows. The Grand Salon oozes elegance and flaunts an inviting Louis XV sofa for couples to nuzzle into. Owner Pascal Gimel and his team (we loved the friendly barman) treat guests to seamless service.

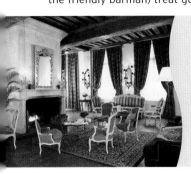

C'est si bon!

Chic and boutique – with the best of Saint Germain on the doorstep.

Bon repos Pick one of the wood-beamed bedrooms – some with half-tester beds reclining under eaves – tricked out with quality soft furnishings and Porthault linens. Soundproofed quarters are matched by stylish marbled bathrooms where Hermès unguents await.

Bon appetit Start the day with breakfast in the pretty Tapestry Room (a woven masterpiece runs along one wall). Linger in the courtyard with a champagne cocktail come spring or summer, or sip a warming cognac by the Grand Salon's fireplace when nights draw in. Light suppers are served in Café Laurent (there's live jazz here on some nights) while a galaxy of restaurants twinkle nearby.

Bon temps You're a few minutes' walk from Pont Neuf, the city's oldest bridge, so soak up its classic views of top sights such as Tour Eiffel and Notre Dame. (And who can ever get enough of Saint Germain!). Leaf through the second-hand books of the bouquinistes along the Seine.

Bon voyage Nearest metro: Saint Michel, Odéon.

tel Millésime

Jacob
Paris
Tel: +33 (0) 1 44 07 97 97
Fax: +33 (0) 1 46 34 55 97
reservation@millesimehotel.com
www.millesimehotel.com

Rooms and rates
22 rooms
Double room for 2 people
per night from €180 to €215
Breakfast from €12

Director
Romain Trollet

Open
All year round

Recent renovations of this handsome 17th century townhouse in the heart of the Left Bank have turned a small slice of Saint Germain into a colourful helping of Provence with all the big-city trimmings. It retains the original staircase but broad-brush strokes of characteristic blues, reds, golds and oranges encourage thoughts of the sunnier Med, carried through into a captivating terracotta painted courtyard with sub-tropical plantings. On balmy days or come dusk it's just the place for a tryst over aperitifs. Staff are solicitous about their guests' enjoyment, and the best of Paris is right outside. A terrific little find.

C'est si bon!

Right pretty Left Bank address.

Bon repos Blues and sunshine yellows predominate in the 22 nicely decorated rooms, making them guaranteed to cheer the greyest day. They're soundproofed and a decent size too, and some at the rear have views over the pretty courtyard (doubly cheering when the magnolia tree is in full bloom).

Bon appetit Breakfast (brought to your room if you prefer) is served in the vaulted breakfast room, where russet slip-covered chairs contrast smartly with whitewashed brick walls. Don't forget to dally in the charming courtyard for a kir or three.

Bon temps No apologies for banging on about the Left Bank's charisma - it's manifestly palpable, and the Millésime is right in the thick of things. Mooch around antique shops, galleries and trendy boutiques, pop into an église or two, or hang out in cute cafés and jazz clubs. There's enough street buzz to make lovers dance down 'em.

Bon voyage Nearest metro: Odéon, St Germain des Prés.

Relais Christine

3 rue Christine
75006 Paris
Tel: +33 (0) 1 40 51 60 80
Fax: +33 (0) 1 40 51 60 81
contact@relais-christine.com
www.relais-christine.com

Rooms and rates
51 rooms
Double room for 2 people
per night from €335 to €430
Breakfast from €20-25

General Manager
Jean-Luc Chomat

Open
All year round

Who doesn't love Saint-Germain-des-Prés, with its arty chocolate box charm and lingering whiff of Gaulois-smoking, Sartre-spouting intellectuals. We love it for the Relais Christine, tucked down the end of a narrow little street. This was originally an Augustinian college built by Saint Louis in 1231, then converted centuries later into a typically grand Parisian mansion with gated courtyard to the front and garden behind. It's sophisticated yet cosy: all beams and panelling, rugs over flagstones, interesting furniture, crackling fires. And the stylish new spa, in the basement vaults, is quite something.

C'est si bon!

Sleek Left Bank bolt-hole with brand new spa.

Bon repos Rooms are individual and intimate, decorated in modern country house style. Plump perhaps for these little numbers: Chambre 54's restful duck-egg blue and yellow; the oak beams and toile de Jouy of 56; the garden-view terrace of the strikingly decorated duplex.

Bon appetit Breakfasting in the 13th century vaulted cellar brings with it quite an atmosphere: uplighters flood ancient whitewashed brick walls and a knight-in-armour stands guard over coffee and croissants. The concierge helpfully steers guests to the right Left Bank restaurants for dinner (avoiding les traps touristiques!).

Bon temps Paris's great sights need no introduction but some of us prefer a little hand-holding: lean on the concierge's recommendations. He will fix special Seine cruises, private guided walking tours, access to hot ticket restaurants and shows and maybe even share some insider tips on enjoying la vie parisienne.

Bon voyage Nearest metro: Odéon.

Château de Brécourt

27120 Pacy-sur-Eure
Tel: +33 (0) 2 32 52 40 50
Fax: +33 (0) 2 32 52 69 65
brécourt@leshotelsparticuliers.com
www.chateaudebrecourt.com

Rooms and rates
25 rooms, 5 apartments
Double room for 2 people
per night from €75 to €261
Breakfast €13. Dinner from €38-58

Proprietors
Les Hôtels Particuliers - Groupe Savry
Manager: Sylvain Choblet

Open
All year round

Oak-beamed ceilings throughout this Louis XVIII château render it both imposing and intimate. Other nice features – mellowed parquet, stone and tiled floors, gigantic chimney pieces (where fires burn merrily on cold nights) and a comfortable mix of furniture from different periods – remain intact. The château is enveloped in 20 hectares of verdant parkland and is approached by a long drive to a front courtyard. Topiary bushes on either side are clipped to echo its pointed turrets, while a small moat adds to the alluring scene. All this, and you're just an hour's drive away from Paris.

C'est si bon!

Illustrious address at the crossroads of Normandy and Ile de France.

Bon repos Some rooms are the stuff of fantasies: bold vermillion walls contrasting with sky-blue drapes and hearths huge enough to play hide-and-seek in; or pastelly pale shades with dramatic criss-cross beams casting shadows from uplighters. All quite theatrical.

Bon appetit Striking red silk-lined and Louis XVI wood panelled rooms set the tone for sophisticated dining. Guests can gorge on the aptly named Grand Siècle menu – a multi-course epicurean feast – on Fridays. When the gods allow, breakfasting al fresco on the terrace, with its grand vistas, is a must.

Bon temps Bliss out in the indoor pool and jacuzzi, with its raftered ceiling and muralled walls. There's golf, riding, tennis and parkland to be discovered, not to mention other châteaux in the Vexin region. Don't miss Monet's gardens at Giverny... pretty as an oil painting.

Bon voyage From the A13: take exit 16 to Vernon or D181 towards Pacy-sur-Eure, then follow signs to Douains.

Cazaudehore et la Forestière

1 avenue Kennedy
78100 Saint-Germain-en-Laye
Tel: +33 (0) 1 39 10 38 38
Fax: +33 (0) 1 39 73 73 88
cazaudehore@relaischateaux.com
www.cazaudehore.fr

Rooms and rates
25 rooms, 5 suites
Double room for 2 people
per night from €185 to €260
Breakfast €15. Dinner from €75

Proprietors
Philippe and Isabelle Cazaudehore

Open
All year round

Just the place if you want to be close to Paris's pulsating city life but stay a step away from its frenetic heartbeat. Sat on the edge of the Saint-Germain-en-Laye forest, this hotel is a picture of calm surrounded by trees and mother nature. It feels like a country home, which indeed it is to Philippe and Isabelle Cazaudehore, the third generation of a family who have nurtured it from modest beginnings 75 years ago. It certainly doesn't stint in putting on the style today, and it's most convivial. The owners say life here follows the rhythm, seasons and colours of Ile de France skies. And we'd say it's never gloomy when skies are grey.

C'est si bon!

Close to the city, but its countryside perch is capital too.

Bon repos Individually appointed rooms are spick 'n' span: all enjoy contemporary and crisp design in soft colours, replete with expected comforts. Some have balconies, others terraces; perfect spots for breakfast on sunny days.

Bon appetit Chef Gregory Galland takes inspiration from the family's south-west origins, creating traditional and imaginative cuisine. Salivate over baked foie gras in a hot wine marinade; parsley risotto with snails; crumbled game quenelles. The cellars hold 50,000 bottles, many of which are exceptional. Dine under the acacias in summer.

Bon temps Saint-Germain is certainly worth a look, with quaint old buildings, cobbled streets and squares alongside modern architecture. Museums are devoted to antiquities, symbolism and Debussy, while the biggest open-air shopping area outside Paris is a short drive away. There are beautiful gardens nearby and access to a health club.

Bon voyage Take the A13 from Paris, then the RN186 for Saint-Germain and N184 towards Pontoise.

Grand Hôtel Barrière

85 rue du Général de Gaulle
95880 Enghien-les-Bains
Tel: +33 (0) 1 39 34 10 00
Fax: +33 (0) 1 39 34 10 01
grandhotelenghien@lucienbarriere.com
www.grand-hotel-enghien.com

Rooms and rates
36 rooms, 7 suites
Double room for 2 people
per night from €150 to €270
Breakfast €18. Dinner from €45

General manager
Frédéric Vincent

Open
All year round

It might seem unusual to visit Ile-de-France and opt to stay in a resort hotel, but quelle surprise! Think big ponds and leafy glades: this smart 50s property overlooks a splendid 100-acre lake in Enghien-les-Bains, next to the Seine and the Oise, and not far from Paris. Behind its distinctive red awnings, the recently renovated interior mixes clubbiness with elegance. It's easy to find yourself unwinding in this restful setting, surrounded by expanses of water, a garden filled with geraniums and lush countryside beyond. Urban sophistication is not far away, though – save some euros for a flutter in the top-class casino nearby.

C'est si bon!

A place for R&R and roulette just 20 minutes from Paris.

Bon repos Recent and attractive refurbishment has given rooms up-to-the-minute comforts. All enjoy lake or garden views. Fingers crossed you're among the guests who sink into their mattress dreaming of how to blow their evening's Blackjack winnings.

Bon appetit L'Aventurine restaurant offers elegant surroundings in which to enjoy the chef's celebrations of traditional French cuisine, alongside a well-stocked wine list. Fine weather sees meals served on the shady terrace, which opens on to the garden.

Bon temps Walk by the lake; dip into forests, and the countryside of Auvers-sur-Oise poetically captured by Monet and Van Gogh; explore the historic abbeys of Royaumont and Notre-Dame-la-Royale; go horseracing; play nine and 18 hole golf; and play your hand in the casino, one of France's best.

Bon voyage Take exit 3 (Saint-Denis) from the A1, and pass through Epinay-sur-Seine to reach Enghien.

Château d'Ermenonville

60950 Ermenonville
Tel: +33 (0) 3 44 54 00 26
Fax: +33 (0) 3 44 54 01 00
ermenonville@leshotelsparticuliers.com
www.chateau-ermenonville.com

Rooms and rates
38 rooms, 11 suites
Double room for 2 people
per night from €75 to €270
Breakfast €13. Dinner from €33-79

Proprietors
Les Hôtels Particuliers - Groupe Savry
Manager: Stéphane Zabotti

Open
All year round

You'd never imagine that this moated extravaganza is just a short hop from Paris's Roissy airport. A classical U-shaped 18th century château, it's the former seat of the Marquis de Girardin, and a fine example of France's contribution to courtly life. Turreted at four corners, it majestically surveys acres of parkland and woods, and to its rear, a moat gives way to a gently curving lake. Its beauty inspired Jean-Jacques Rousseau to spend his last days here, though today's guests need only expire with delight at the lavishly composed interior. Staff believe strongly in the philosophy of good service.

C'est si bon!

Somewhere to stir the soul - as it did for the philosopher Rousseau.

Bon repos Boudoirs enjoy the full château treatment: lofty ceilings, tall windows, polished parquet, marble chimney pieces, opulent mirrors, fine furniture and downy soft beds. Suites - some of them big enough to set sail in - are swisher still.

Bon appetit Tables are nicely spaced within the elegant confines of the restaurant La Table du Poète, so diners can coo sweet nothings - in verse of course - without being overheard. Traditional northern French dishes and modern cuisine demonstrate good poetic virtues. Lunch is served on the terrace in good weather.

Bon temps Strolling past the lake on the velvety green lawns should delight the senses (as it did for J-J R). Alternatively, you can saddle up or play tennis and golf. Picturesque diversions close by include Chantilly and the medieval village of Senlis.

Bon voyage Arriving from the north (A1): take exit 8 to Chantilly/Senlis. The N330 then leads to Ermenonville.

Château du Maréchal de Saxe

91330 Yerres
Tel: +33 (0) 1 69 48 78 53
Fax: +33 (0) 1 69 83 84 91
saxe@leshotelsparticuliers.com
www.chateaudumarechaldesaxe.com

Rooms and rates
16 rooms, 2 suites
Double room for 2 people
per night from €122 to €382
Breakfast €13. Dinner from €36-65

Proprietors
Les Hôtels Particuliers - Groupe Savry
Manager: Marie-Christine Bosson

Open
All year round

History runs off the walls of this grandest of residences just 12 miles from Paris. Once the seat of the venerable Marshal of Saxe, whose heroic exploits on the battlefield won him the gratitude of Louis XV, its splendid salons and sweeping gated driveway evoke all the grandeur of the ancien régime. The palatial marble-floored Grand Salon, with its battle trophies and depictions of hunting scenes, is matched by the impressive walled grounds and moated entrance. You can almost imagine your gilded carriage awaiting outside the front door at this elegant address just half an hour from Paris.

C'est si bon!

Blue-blooded château that's a class act.

Bon repos Intimacy has not been lost amid the château's princely splendour. Classic rooms have four-poster or canopied beds and period furniture. Some have fireplaces, beams and polished wood floors, while others have delicately painted wood panelling. Gleaming bathrooms are designed with 21st century comforts in mind.

Bon appetit Top-class cooking in the chandeliered Les Menus Plaisirs restaurant (and out on the terrace in summer) embraces both modern and traditional. Dine on fillet of duck pan-fried with blackcurrants, perhaps, or ballottine of pigeon with truffles and foie gras. Wine selections are spot-on.

Bon temps Paris is a short drive to the north. Discoveries in the vicinity include the Vacherot and Lecoufle orchid farm at Boissy Saint Léger, with its dozens of varieties of exotic plants.

Bon voyage From Paris: leave the city via Porte de Bercy. Take the A4 in the direction of Melun and Provins.

Abbaye des Vaux de Cernay

78720 Cernay-la-Ville
Tel: +33 (0) 1 34 85 23 00
Fax: +33 (0) 1 34 85 11 60
reception.cernay@leshotelsparticuliers.com
www.abbayedecernay.com

Rooms and rates
54 rooms, 3 suites
Double room for 2 people
per night from €96 to €590
Breakfast €14. Dinner from €44-€85

Proprietors
Les Hôtels Particuliers - Groupe Savry
Manager: Aurélien Lecomte

Open
All year round

This former 12th century Cistercian monastery became the home of Baron Nathaniel de Rothschild in the late Victorian era. Carefully restored, it now glows with the patina of grandness, old money and idiosyncratic luxury. Original Gothic backdrops – cloisters, scriptoriums, mystical and medieval flourishes – embellish salon after salon (there are 17 of them), but the building's lofty grandeur and impeccable furnishings (forget about hard pews!) are softened by warm service. Throw in the location – 65 hectares of tended parkland complete with lake – and you have supreme elegance in a palatial setting.

C'est si bon!

Former Rothschild residence reborn from Cistercian abbey... quelle richesse!

Bon repos Sumptuous suites offer acres of space and decoration of impeccable grandeur. The Chambre du Baron James and Suite de la Baronne (with its ensuite wall to wall Art Nouveau oak panelling and recessed marble bath) are spectacular.

Bon appetit The Prior's Table (formerly the monks' refectory) with dramatic vaulted ceiling is laid for Michelin cuisine. A devilishly tempting eight course Menu de Dégustation with flawless wines hardly encourages saintly abstinence. Well-drilled waiters provide seamless service.

Bon temps Indulge in the sybaritic splendour of the fitness centre, spa and pool. Push the boat out across the lake, play tennis, go fishing or horse riding. Guided visits around the grounds reveal more of the abbey's fascinating past, while trips to Breteuil or Versailles unveil another side of France's history.

Bon voyage Exit Paris via Pont de Sèvres for Chartres. Turn on to N306/D906 for Cernay la Ville, then take D24.

La ferme des Vallées

78610 Auffargis
Tel: +33 (0) 1 30 46 32 42
Fax: +33 (0) 1 30 46 32 23
vallees@leshotelsparticuliers.com
www.lafermedesvallees.com

Rooms and rates
28 rooms, 2 suites
Double room for 2 people
per night room €65 to €244
Breakfast €12

Proprietors
Les Hôtels Particuliers - Groupe Savry
Manager: Lavinia Couturier

Open
All year round

What was once a hotchpotch of dilapidated 13th century farmyard buildings and barns used by lay brothers on the domaine of nearby sister hotel Abbaye des Vaux de Cernay has been converted into a sweet and simple addition to the grand house up the road. And 3,000 acres of protected parkland means La Ferme des Vallées is blessed with peace and quiet. A sense of the past has been sympathetically preserved with lots of original beams and exposed stonework, sloping roofs and inglenooks, clean-limbed wood and wicker furniture. What's more, you can count on staff to provide a high order of service.

C'est si bon!

Pastoral peace makes this place a farmhouse favourite.

Bon repos No swagged French windows or fancy four-posters here; the style's clean and country-simple but you won't miss your townie comforts. Bathrooms sport naive animal mosaics on the walls. Shelves are dotted with china ducks and rabbits. Reckon to sleep like lambs.

Bon appetit Meals are taken in the long dining room with attractive stonework running along one side, and windows fronting the pretty courtyard on the other. Breakfast croissants are farmhouse-fresh. If you want to enjoy serious holy orders, make a dinner reservation at the Abbaye's Michelin-starred La Table du Prieur just up the road.

Bon temps The location in the picturesque Chevreuse Valley sets guests up for discovering a whole cavalcade of châteaux in the region. Closer to hand are an outdoor pool and tennis court, plus indoor table tennis. Golf, fishing and riding can be arranged close by.

Bon voyage Leave Paris (45km) on the A10, taking the N10 at Les Ulis past Cernay and Le Perray to Auffargis.

Trianon Palace

1 boulevard de la Reine
78000 Versailles
Tel: +33 (0) 1 30 84 50 00
Fax: +33 (0) 1 30 84 50 01
reservation.01104@westin.com
www.trianonpalace.com

Rooms and rates
166 rooms, 26 suites
Double room for 2 people
per night from €230 to €400
Breakfast €27. Dinner from €60

General manager
Giovanni Caronia

Open
All year round

As if the splendour of the Trianon Palace isn't enough – you can almost imagine the Sun King and his Queen presiding here – there's the magnificent Château de Versailles and surrounding parks beside it, plus a vast spa that caters to every indulgence (very Louis XIV). Stars, statesmen and famous figures have all stayed since it was built a century ago, while more recent refurbishment has added the luxurious new Pavillon. State rooms and salons abound, decorated with aristocratic antiques, Savonnerie carpets, tapestries and chandeliers. It's all kept ticking by an army of flunkies. L'art de vivre rules, and how.

C'est si bon!

One of Paris's leading palace hotels, complete with sumptuous spa.

Bon repos Ever floated on air? You might do just that in suites boasting beds with 900 springs, soft quilts and plump feather pillows. Luxurious baths have dual basins while showers have massage jets.

Bon appetit Gastronomic treats aplenty here as food is overseen by one of France's lauded chefs, Gérard Vie – a recipient of Michelin stars and Gault Millau tocques. There's impeccable haute cuisine in the formal Les Trois Marchés; lighter dishes in the Café Trianon; intimacy in the 20-seater Petits Marchés; and cocktails in the Bar Marie-Antoinette (snacks too, but there's no need to eat cake!)

Bon temps Enjoy red carpet treatment: the concierge can arrange private visits to the Château and the royal chapel. Explore the Great and Small Trianon parks, royal vineyard, stables and antique shops. Sports include six golf courses, riding, shooting and rowing on the Grand Canal.

Bon voyage From Paris: join the A13, and leave at Exit 5 marked Versailles Centre. Turn right into Blvd de la Reine.

The Loire Valley:
In and around château country

Aller for rivers of romance
Manger crottin de Chavignol – local goat's cheese
Santé! Chilled Vouvray, Sancerre and Pouilly-Fumé

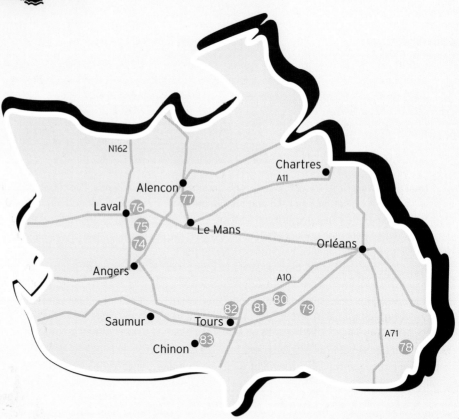

River Loire ———
Roads ———

Pages 74 – 83

Why?

Come here for castles, castles, castles... from the Renaissance to the Rabelaisian, the feudal to the fairytale. These architectural jewels, with the famous river lapping at their feet, evoke a courtly age of knights, kings and courtesans. Steeped in royal history and intrigue, they have inspired artists and literary giants over the ages. Vine-clad landscapes and glinting water create a sumptuous setting.

So why not...♥

- Float down the Loire by boat to absorb its splendour
- Lose yourself in the maze at Château de Chenonceau
- Pedal through miles of cycle paths at Château de Chaubord
- See the gardens in full bloom at Château de Villandry
- Wander through the wine towns of Blois, Chinon and Sancerre

Château des Briottières

49330 Champigné
Tel: +33 (0) 2 41 42 00 02
Fax: +33 (0) 2 41 42 01 55
briottieres@wanadoo.fr
www.briottieres.com

Rooms and rates
16 rooms
Double room for 2 people
per night from €120 to €240
Breakfast €11. Dinner from €46

Proprietors
François and Hedwige de Valbray

Open
All year except 2 weeks at
Christmas and in February

Built in 1773 and the Valbray family home since 1820, this blissful Anjou château stands in 50 hectares of English-style parkland, its tranquillity ruffled only by swans gliding across the lake. It has all the lazy charm of an olden-days aristocratic house party, hosted by the sociable and hospitable François and Hedwige de Valbray. While away a summer's afternoon on the tennis courts, or borrow a bicycle to explore bucolic Loire villages. After dinner, pop along to the library for a game of billiards, or simply sip an Armagnac beneath the twinkling chandeliers of the antique-laden salons.

C'est si bon!

Divine Loire château with tones of Merchant Ivory.

Bon repos Bedrooms in the main house are bright and airy, with views across the gardens, lake or chapel. There's been a feminine hand at work in La Chambre Rose, with its swathes of floral curtains framing beds and windows. Rooms in the old Orangerie are more restrained, while bathrooms are extravagantly sized.

Bon appetit Tables draped in sumptuous linen are decked with gleaming silver candelabra and a battery of glasses ready for quaffing crisp Anjou wines. Book in advance for a true gourmet feast using traditional family recipes and fresh, seasonal ingredients.

Bon temps Feast your senses on the lavish Loire Valley châteaux; visit the great abbeys of Solesmes and Fontevraud; pound the streets of medieval Angers or simply laze along the river in a canoe. The Breton coast and Mont Saint Michel are easy day trips.

Bon voyage From Paris: take the A11 to Exit 11 (Durtal). Join the D768 for Daumeray and Châteauneuf-sur-Sarthe.

Prieuré de la Gilardière

53200 Gennes-sur-Glaize
Tel: +33 (0) 2 43 70 93 03
Fax: +33 (0) 2 43 70 93 03
lagilar@hotmail.com
(no website)

Rooms and rates
4 rooms
Double room for 2 people
per night from €55 to €100
Breakfast included. Dinner €25

Proprietors
Ghislain and Françoise Drion

Open
1 May - 31 October

Standing proud near the village of Gennes sur Glaize just north of the Loire Valley, this former monastic priory is still visibly cloaked in history. Back in the 15th century, it was a resting place for religious pilgrims en route to Santiago di Compostella in Spain. Later, following the French revolution, it was turned into a sumptuous home for land-owning aristocrats. Its present owners have ensured that the priory's conversion into a magnificent country residence has preserved many of its finest original features: character is blessed with contemporary comforts. Impressive grounds set it off a treat.

C'est si bon!

Confess to indulgence in this peaceful old Loire priory.

Bon repos With just four bedrooms, the priory feels like an intimate and exclusive country retreat. Forget spartan conditions; these cells are furnished with taste and rich antique ornamentation. Beams and old Tuffeau fireplaces invite indulgent relaxation.

Bon appetit Breakfast awaits in a country-style dining room complete with rafters, huge hearth and checked tablecloth. Look forward to home-made jams, organic bread and farm produce to awaken those tastebuds, while local restaurateurs offer the best of cuisine du terroir at night.

Bon temps With over 170 acres of young plantations here, you'll feel as if you're in open country. There's a tennis court and swimming pool in the grounds, and a games room with billiard table for cooler weather. Further afield, try fishing, golf, riding, guided walks and kayaking.

Bon voyage From Laval: take the N162/D28 to Château Gontier and Gennes-sur-Glaize. Turn right for Bierné, then left for La Gilardière at St Aignan.

Le Bas du Gast

6 rue de la Halle aux Toiles
53000 Laval
Tel: +33 (0) 2 43 49 22 79
Fax: +33 (0) 2 43 56 44 71
chateaubasdugast@wanadoo.fr
www.chateauxandcountry.com

Rooms and rates
4 rooms
Double room for 2 people
per night from €110 to €200
Breakfast from €13-18

Proprietor
François Williot

Open
1 January - 30 November

It's hard to believe that this splendid mansion in Laval - an old fortified town on the edge of the Loire - was bought as a near-wreck in the 60s. After decades of neglect, the former residence of one of the Sun King's henchmen has now been brilliantly restored to its former glory thanks to the TLC and tenacity of Jules-Emile Williot, whose son François is now custodian of this jewel in the town's architectural crown. Standing proud behind its original baroque box garden, Le Bas du Gast now offers a taste of aristocratic France - and as guests in the châtelain's own home, you won't want for comfort. Try to arrive by 8pm.

C'est si bon!

Upper-crust chambre
d'hôte with bags of style.

Bon repos No expense has been spared in the château's careful restoration. Tinted hand-carved wooden wall panelling, crested marble fireplaces and authentic window hangings are set off by elegant period furniture. A grand granite staircase with ornate balustrade leads up to the spacious and understated guestrooms.

Bon appetit Breakfast - continental or à l'anglais - is served in the grand parquet-floored dining room. Laval has plenty of good restaurants and your hosts are happy to suggest some good dining spots for the evening.

Bon temps You're at the crossroads of Normandy, Brittany and the Loire here. After a foray into Loire château country, hire bikes for a spin in country lanes, swim or play tennis. Explore medieval Sainte-Suzanne, swing a golf club on nearby fairways, or go canoeing on the River Mayenne.

Bon voyage From Paris: take A81 to Laval and cross to the right bank of the river. Bas du Gast is signed from there and is not far from the cathedral, close to the Salle Polyvalente.

Château de Saint-Paterne

72610 Saint Paterne
Sarthe
Tel: +33 (0) 2 33 27 54 71
Fax: +33 (0) 2 33 29 16 71
paterne@club-internet.fr
www.chateau-saintpaterne.com

Rooms and rates
8 rooms
Double room for 2 people
per night from €105 to €210
Breakfast €10. Dinner from €40

Proprietors
Charles-Henry and Ségolène de Valbray

Open
April - December

This jewel of a Renaissance château boasts some perfect credentials as a romantic hideaway – it's where 15th century King Henry IV tucked away his lovers, far from the prying eyes of the court. And you can see why. Wrapped in lavish 25-acre gardens and vibrantly restored by Charles-Henry and Ségolène de Valbray, the rooms are a welcoming mix of family heirlooms and sunny Mediterranean colours. It's a place to get lost among the rafters, nooks and crannies of the attic rooms, to lounge on the terrace and have a dip in the pool on balmy summer days, or to huddle up warm and toasty beside a roaring fire on chilly autumn nights.

C'est si bon!

Old Loire lovenest with refreshing southern style

Bon repos Match your room to your mood, whether it's the wood-panelled grandeur of Chambre du Maréchal, the floral canopied bed of the sprawling Chambre de la Roseraie or the heavy rough-cut roof beams of Chambre de la Tour.

Bon appetit Get ready for some liaisons délicieuses over dinner in the formal dining room, its rich red drapes warmed by flickering candlelight. Expect flavoursome traditional French fare using vegetables freshly picked from the château's own kitchen garden. Petit déjeuner is prettily served in the old kitchens.

Bon temps Explore the Perche, a region of mellow manor houses, lush forests and bijou villages. Within easy day-trip distance are Sées cathedral and a clutch of Loire Valley châteaux, Mont Saint Michel and Normandy's D-Day beaches. Trawl for local antiques, or stock up on cider, Calvados and Normandy cheeses at the medieval market in Mamers.

Bon voyage From Tours: take the A28 to Le Mans and Alençon (Exit 19), then D311 and follow signs for St Paterne.

Château d'Ivoy

18380 Ivoy-le-Pré
Tel: +33 (0) 2 48 58 85 01
Fax: +33 (0) 2 48 58 85 02
chateau.divoy@wanadoo.fr
http://perso.wanadoo.fr/chateau.divoy

Rooms and rates
6 rooms
Double room for 2 people
per night from €140 to €195
Breakfast included

Proprietors
Marie-France Gouëffon-de Vaivre

Open
All year round

History has blazed a colourful trail through this handsome château, set in a sea of greenery at the gates of Sancerre country. Once home to Mary Queen of Scot's treasurer (the Scottish clan had a summer house down the road), it has now been transformed by well-travelled interior decorator Marie-France Gouëffon-de-Vaivre. Supremely elegant rooms reflect her cosmopolitan savoir-vivre, with an eclectic mix of rare objets d'art, tapestries and statuary. Shades of the château's Celtic past survive, with flourishes of tweeds and tartans, while sofa cushions covered in canine portraits add unexpected flashes of humour. The result is stunning.

C'est si bon!

Flair and flamboyance in a delectable Loire château.

Bon repos Each of the six canopied bedrooms has its own rich personality: you can slumber amid shades of Kipling, Lord Drummond, La Fayette or Le Grand Meaulnes. One four-poster bears the arms of Queen Victoria, while toile de Jouy linens, antique washstands, beautifully coordinated fabrics and even (in Kipling) Indian mosquito nets add visual interest. Tall windows capture the lovely grounds outside.

Bon appetit Breakfast is served around a large oak table in the richly decorated dining room, with its dark walls and oil paintings. There's no shortage of good places to dine out in the vicinity, and your hosts are happy to advise.

Bon temps You'll find a billiard table, piano, croquet lawn and pool here, while shooting trips are easily arranged. Beyond the gates, the cathedral at Bourges, the porcelain museum and shop at Foëcy and the vineyards of Sancerre await discovery.

Bon voyage From Orléans: take the A71 to Salbris (Exit 4), D944/D926 to la Chapelle d'Angillon and D12 to Ivoy le Pré.

Château de Chissay

41400 Montrichard, Loir-et-Cher
Tel: +33 (0) 2 54 32 32 01
Fax: +33 (0) 2 54 32 43 80
chissay@leshotelsparticuliers.com
www.chateaudechissay.com

Rooms and rates
22 rooms, 10 suites
Double room for 2 people
per night from €121 to €265
Breakfast €13. Dinner from €33-52

Proprietors
Les Hôtels Particuliers - Groupe Savry
Manager: Alain Guinoiseau

Open
Mid March - Mid November

Chissay looks glorious, set in 25 acres of forested parkland. One guest remarked that the château doesn't simply trade on its history but actually delivers the goods – and who are we to disagree? It was started in the 13th century, then enlarged in the Renaissance, with fairytale turrets and a chapel in the main tower. It thus covers the full span of classic Touraine architecture. What's more, Charles VII and Louis XI once lived there, as did dashing ducs, and General de Gaulle prior to dashing to Britain in WWII. And the goods? It's stylish yet relaxed, service doesn't stint, and there's a belief that the guest is king (or queen). Voilà!

C'est si bon!

Once home to French royals – and guests still get the royal treatment.

Bon repos Tranquillity is the common characteristic of these individually decorated rooms, some four-postered, and all with views. Many bathrooms have mosaics depicting figures from the château's colourful past. The real surprise is the Troglodyte suite carved out of solid rock – surreal and surprisingly comfortable.

Bon appetit La Table du Roy, Chissay's part-panelled and vaulted Gothic restaurant, comes with well-dressed and generously spaced tables, needlepoint chairs and soft lighting to positively encourage... Roymance. Linger over a lavish gourmet menu and a glass or three of Vouvray.

Bon temps The Loire Valley means châteaux... and then some. If you can only visit a couple then Chenonceau and Amboise, on the doorstep, are jewels in the crown. Gorgeous countryside for riding, fishing, cycling and picnicking. Don't forget the hotel's heated pool.

Bon voyage From Paris: exit A10 at Blois, cross the Loire, follow signs to Vierzon, and join D764 for Montrichard.

Château de Pray

37400 Amboise
Indre-et-Loire
Tel: +33 (0) 2 47 57 23 67
Fax: +33 (0) 2 47 57 32 50
praycastel@online.fr
http://praycastel.online.fr

Rooms and rates
17 rooms, 2 apartments
Double room for 2 people
per night from €95 to €165
Breakfast €11. Dinner from €41

General manager
Graziella Laurenty

Open
22 Jan - 15 Nov and 1-31 Dec

As châteaux go this may be smaller than some but, perched above the Loire and surrounded by bosky woods, it's every bit as gorgeous. Built in the 13th century as a stronghold (it boasts the classic turrets) it first became a residence in the Renaissance, then home to various royal courtiers, later housing a colleague of La Fayette, the writer Alphonse Daudet and, apparently, a friendly ghost. Elements of its long and colourful history are reflected in stylish furnishings and idiosyncratic artefacts, lending the place a wholly delightful atmosphere. All this, and the vineyards of Chinon and Vouvray close by. Pray enjoy.

C'est si bon!

Stunning medieval fortress with glorious views over the Loire.

Bon repos 19 traditionally decorated guest rooms include some with four-posters draped with elegant chintz. Bag a room if you can with uninterrupted views across manicured lawns towards the river (this helps the course of true love run smooth). Good marble bathrooms too.

Bon appetit A magnificent full-length tapestry and massive stone hearth overlook pretty, formally-laid tables. Gourmets have a choice of two prix-fixe menus or à la carte dining, offering deliciously light or elaborate cooking. Everything's delivered fresh each day from the potager.

Bon temps It's château heaven hereabouts. Places within easy reach include Amboise, Chambord and Blois – the seat of kings; Chenonceau, spanning the river; Loches, where Joan of Arc met Charles VII; Villandry; with its great gardens; and Clos Lucé, home of Da Vinci.

Bon voyage Take the D31 for Amboise at exit 18 on the A10. After the bridge, turn right towards Chargé and right again at stop sign. The château is second on the right.

Château de Noizay

Route de Chançay
37210 Noizay
Tel: +33 (0) 2 47 52 11 01
Fax: +33 (0) 2 47 52 04 64
noizay@relaischateaux.com
www.chateaudenoizay.com

Rooms and rates
19 rooms
Double room for 2 people
per night from €135 to €265
Breakfast €17. Dinner from €47

Proprietor
François Mollard

Open
Mid March - mid January

The neat symmetrical proportions, sweeping manicured lawns and bucolic parkland of this bijou 16th century château are a delight. On entering, you'll be greeted by an impressive wood balustrade where knights in armour stand guard on either side of a huge stained glass window. Noizay has historical antecedents: it was here that the leader of an anti-monarchist conspiracy was caught plotting in 1560. Fine antique furniture is polished to a fault, surfaces everywhere glint warmly. Outside, there's a charming pool with loungers. The only conspiracy today is between staff who contrive to ensure guests' utter enjoyment.

C'est si bon!

Intimately scaled Loire château with lashings of style.

Bon repos Think boudoir. Rooms are exquisitely done out with draped bedheads, floaty fabrics or toile de Jouy, vases of lilies, delicate period furniture and garden views. Two rooms in a separate building, The Clockhouse, offer nights in scarlet coloured surrounds with a king-size four-poster, lover's chest, whirlpool bath and private garden.

Bon appetit Two softly lit dining rooms and a terrace (sunlit by day) offer gastronomy featuring seasonal Touraine specialities matched by spiffing Loire wines. Food is well presented on the plate (and delivers no less on the palate). Enjoy aperitifs and post prandials in the library.

Bon temps Absorb the Loire's fabulous scenery, Vouvray vineyards and royal châteaux by hot air balloon or helicopter (ascend and descend from the hotel grounds). Or try walking and biking; canoeing and boating; riding; playing tennis and golfing.

Bon voyage From A10: take D31 (Exit 18) to Amboise, and N152 to Tours. Join the D78 to Noizay 6km after Amboise.

Les Hautes Roches

86 quai de la Loire, 37210
Rochecorbon, Indre-et-Loire
Tel: +33 (0) 2 47 52 88 88
Fax: +33 (0) 2 47 52 81 30
hautes.roches@wanadoo.fr
www.leshautesroches.com

Rooms and rates
15 rooms
Double room for 2 people
per night from €125 to €255
Breakfast €17. Dinner €56-70

Proprietor
Philippe Mollard

Open
Mid March - late January

If you've ever fancied bedding down in an old troglodyte cave, this is the place to do it in style. The aptly named Les Hautes Roches embraces the caves themselves (carved from medieval rock quarries) and an 18th century château, all done up with irrepressible Val de Loire style. Located bang on the banks of the Loire with uninterrupted river views and surrounded by Vouvray's famous vineyards, the hotel has a gorgeous terrace, part shaded by lime trees and overlooking pretty gardens. A pleasingly landscaped swimming pool sits amid lush greenery skirted by the river. This lovely little place really rocks.

C'est si bon!

Just the place to bring out those caveman instincts.

Bon repos One-time monastic cells have been turned into supremely comfortable rooms, some with rough-hewn walls and ceilings that retain a sense of the original (just don't drag your partner to bed by the hair). Luxurious soft furnishings, airy windows and modern bathrooms meanwhile ensure you won't miss your creature comforts.

Bon appetit The dining room - prettily painted in yellow and coral with windows overlooking the water - is the place to catch chef Didier Edon's sublime all-lobster menu, or cuisine du terroir. Breakfast (and dinner on warm evenings) is served on what is arguably the river's finest terrace.

Bon temps Chill out on all the Loire châteaux your heart desires: they're right here on the doorstep. Take a guided tour of the mile-long Marc Brédif wine caves nearby - just the place to try a nicely chilled glass of local Saumur - or cool off in summer in that pool.

Bon voyage From the A10 motorway, take exit 20 for Tours - Sainte Radegonde, then turn left towards Vouvray.

Château de Marçay

37500 Chinon
Tel: +33 (0) 2 47 93 03 47
Fax: +33 (0) 2 47 93 45 33
marcay@relaischateaux.com
www.chateaudemarcay.com

Rooms and rates
30 rooms, 4 suites
Double room for 2 people
per night from €114 to €290
Breakfast €18. Dinner from €46

General manager
Bernard Beteille

Open
Mid March - Mid January

The centuries-old and history-rich Château de Marçay, near Chinon - with its salt-cellar towers, formal gardens, lake and parklands - is a fine example of a Loire des res. It certainly has presence. Rabelais declared its landscape enchanting, and today's visitors won't disagree. Within its stout walls, ancient panelling and beams form a backdrop to antique-filled salons and private lounges, one with a huge and inviting fireplace. What's more, the château bottles its own wine, runs its own bakery, boasts a top-class restaurant and has a rather lovely pool. Marçay certainly makes a splash.

C'est si bon!

Wonderful looking château which bottles its own vin de Loire (belle cave too!).

Bon repos Guests should relish being banished to the tower here. Some rooms have been done up in bright and uplifting colour schemes, with wallpaper and sumptuous soft furnishings tastefully coordinated. Beds are wide and welcoming with lots of pillows. Bathrooms (some of them huge) are well kitted out. Terrific views, too.

Bon appetit New chef Marc de Passorio continues the elegant restaurant's inestimable reputation. His signature dishes include Géline Dame Noire with orange juniper; fillet of fried perch with the château's wine vinaigrette, baby leeks and chanterelles; and stuffed pigeon with blackthorn juice. Fine Loire vintages are naturally on hand.

Bon temps Chinon is a venerable fortress town, so explore; follow the Loire's historic châteaux roots; laze by the pool or have a dip after a morning's mountain-biking, riding, canoeing, tennis or golf; visit vineyards and cellars.

Bon voyage Take the A10 from Paris, exit at Sainte Maure de Touraine, then take the D 760 to Chinon (follow arrows).

The Atlantic coast:
From Biarritz to past Ile de Ré

Aller for surf 'n' turf
Manger fresh oysters
Santé! St Emilion and Bordeaux claret

87

A10

Ile de Ré 86 • La Rochelle

Saintes

88

89

Bordeaux • 91 90

92

A62

N10

93-
99 • Biarritz
• Guéthary
St. Jean de Luz

A64

Rivers
Roads

Pages 86 – 99

Why?

Less crowded than the Côte d'Azur, France's Atlantic coast - known for its miles of powdery sands - is an underrated gem. From the island outpost of Ile de Ré in the North - a summer refuge for chic Parisians - to the surfing beaches of Biarritz in the South, this is a place for ocean-fresh seafood, wild birds and sand dunes. You're also on the doorstep of the famous Bordeaux vineyards and France's cognac region.

So why not...♥

- Watch the oyster boats landing their daily catch
- Take to a boogie board when the surf's up
- Play footsie in the quayside cafés of La Rochelle
- Tee off against the backdrop of the Pyrenees
- Window shop in the chic boutiques of Biarritz and Saint-Jean-de-Luz

Domaine de la Baronnie

21 rue Baron de Chantal
17410 Saint-Martin de Ré
Tel: +33 (0) 5 46 09 21 29
Fax: +33 (0) 5 46 09 95 29
info@domainedelabaronnie.com
www.domainedelabaronnie.com

Room and rates
6 rooms
Double room for 2 people
per night from €140 to €195
Breakfast €12

Proprietors
Pierre and Florence Pallardy

Open
Easter – end October

Pierre and Florence Pallardy have turned La Baronnie, their turreted 18th century mansion once owned by Louis XVI on the island-jewel of Ile de Ré, into a temple of well-being. Florence has decorated with refinement, with period antiques, Persian rugs and kelims, and sumptuous fabrics. Pierre, an osteopath and dietician, provides therapeutic massage and a range of special treatments. Outside, a spruce and sheltered garden joins a cobbled courtyard lined with heady honeysuckle, jasmin and oleander. Such serene surroundings, and Pierre's expert ministrations, work wonders on the psyche. It's pure pleasure, too.

C'est si bon!

Island haven for unwinding and re-energising.

Bon repos Beautifully decorated chambres have evocative names, so you could get acquainted with Monsieur de Beauséjour or Madame de Sévigné. Each possesses its own allure, whether it's a richly draped canopied bed, views over the pretty flowered garden, or characterful containment in one of the towers.

Bon appetit Breakfast in the airy dining room or lush garden is a feast: tables are laden with cheeses, fruits and yoghurts, breads and jams. You won't go hungry at night, either, with ocean-fresh seafood on the menu du jour in the island's many restaurants.

Bon temps There's Saint Martin's eye-catching harbour, citadel and museum to discover, not to mention terrific beaches: miles and miles of peachy sand and dunes. This is a place to get the wind in your hair and take up seasports and cycling; pedal away with non-stop views of the waves.

Bon voyage From La Rochelle: take the N11 causeway (toll) to Saint-Martin de Ré.

Hôtel du Général d'Elbée

85330 Noirmoutier en l'Isle
Tel: +33 (0) 2 51 39 10 29
Fax: +33 (0) 2 51 39 08 23
elbee@leshotelsparticuliers.com
www.generaldelbee.com

Rooms and rates
23 rooms, 4 apartments
Double room for 2 people
per night from €96 to €277
Breakfast €12

Proprietors
Les Hôtels Particuliers - Groupe Savry
Managers: O. Savry and C. Lamiaud

Open
April – September

You cross a little causeway to the Ile de Noirmoutier to reach this solid stone building set firmly on the quayside, where tiny craft are beached when the tide's out. In fine weather it's fun to sit on the first-floor terrace and watch the bustle in the harbour and yachts bobbing on the waves. A revolutionary uprising was planned within these 18th century walls and the hapless General d'Elbée dispatched by firing squad for his royalist sympathies. What tales these bricks could tell! Today, the stone-flagged, oak-beamed and country-inspired interior, with its fresh flowers and antiques, is all sweetness and light.

C'est si bon!

Revolutionaries plotted here – you'll only lose your head to its charms.

Bon repos Recently decorated rooms – some with high-beamed ceilings – feel inviting and fresh. Some have full-length windows with balconies and harbour views, while others overlook the pool and garden. Nice bathrooms, too.

Bon appetit Breakfast is served in-house, and staff are happy to book you a table for dinner at L'Atlantide, the restaurant of sister hotel Punta Lara, just over a mile away. Catch of the day (invariably brill!) could well be locally landed crab, lobster or sea bass.

Bon temps There's a pool to laze around in the hotel's courtyard garden. You can watch Atlantic rollers break on long sandy beaches, check out the nearby medieval castle or stride out along windswept salt marshes. Do book excursions and cruises along the coast: this is definitely the place to mess about in boats.

Bon voyage From Nantes: take the D751/D758 to Beauvoir sur Mer. You can drive across to Noirmoutier via Le Gois at low tide; otherwise take the bridge.

The Atlantic coast

Moulin du Val de Seugne

Marcouze
17240 Mosnac
Tel: +33 (0) 5 46 70 46 16
Fax: +33 (0) 5 46 70 48 14
moulin@valdeseugne.com
www.valdeseugne.com

Rooms and rates
10 rooms
Double room for 2 people
per night from €90 to €145
Breakfast €10. Dinner from €19

Proprietors
Jean-Marie Bedin

Open
All year round

This lovely water mill, situated on its own islet, dates back to the 16th century when life was more grinding (they milled flour here), but guests needn't lift a finger except to tickle the crystal-clear Seugne river which gently eddies up to the building's walls. A dense forest of tall ash and little meadows lie opposite the mill; moss, lichen and wild flowers cling to muddy banks and old stone. The place has been stylishly and sympathetically converted into a hotel. Beams, floors and fireplaces remain intact, while clubby leather chairs furnish the salons. The setting's sylvan, its peace broken only by birdsong, and the quacking of ducks.

C'est si bon!

Old converted mill where you're miles from the millstones of reality.

Bon repos Sun and moon reflect through shady saplings onto placid water which almost comes up to the terraces outside. Inside, soothingly decorated, antique-filled rooms (some with canopied beds) await. Breakfast in bed is a treat here.

Bon appetit Pick a table by tall picture windows looking out over the meadows, or a spot on the terrace with water shimmering below. Precede dinner, perhaps, with a Pineau des Charentes aperitif, complement your mains with a smooth Bordeaux, and finish with a Brûlot Charentais liqueur.

Bon temps Grape lovers will want to explore Cognac, Bordeaux and the Médoc vineyards. Anglers can hook carp in the Seugne or trout in the Maine; hedonists may laze in the hotel's pool (or try the aquacentre at Jonzac); while energetic types can opt for tennis, golf and go-karting. Owls after nightlife will find places to party nearby.

Bon voyage From Bordeaux, take exit 37 from A10 and join D730 to Mirambeau. Follow signs to St-Génis and Mosnac.

Château de Mirambeau

17150 Mirambeau
Tel: +33 (0) 5 46 04 91 20
Fax: +33 (0) 5 46 04 26 72
sas.mirambeau@tiscali.fr
www.chateauxmirambeau.com

Rooms and rates
16 rooms, 3 suites
Double room for 2 people
per night from €168 to €378
Breakfast from €21. Dinner from €40

General manager
Eric Hertz

Open
15 March - 30 September

A stay at this imposing château with its late Romanesque architecture - all towers, turrets and spires - makes an ideal starting point for exploring the countryside of Bordeaux and Cognac. Mirambeau commands its own 20 acres of parkland complete with courtyards, walkways, manicured lawns and parterred gardens. Very lordly. The aristocratic ambience continues inside with a richly appointed interior. In the past flunkeys would have been dancing attendance; today the staff seem no less diligent in ensuring guests' whims are attended to. The grand salon is just the spot to linger with a glass of Grand Cru.

C'est si bon!

Château with double the bubble: fabulous wines and champagnes, superb spa.

Bon repos Rooms, some with four-posters, are plush and languorous. Individually decorated with 19th century antiques and period wallpapers, they come with fresh, fully tiled bathrooms. Nothing for it but to loll back in one of those oversized tubs with a flute of fizz.

Bon appetit Dine gastronomically from a table dressed with crystal and silverware. Seafood is good here, accompanied perhaps by a lightly chilled red. Withdraw to the aptly-named Cognathèque afterwards to nurse a golden digestif by the splendid fireplace.

Bon temps Spa pampering here is a must: there's a hammam, sauna and two pools to indulge in. Thus refreshed, stroll through the leafy grounds, survey the impressive surrounds from the terrace or play tennis. And do visit the region's three illustrious towns famous for their libations: Cognac, Bordeaux and St. Emilion.

Bon voyage From Bordeaux: join the A10 north and take Exit 37 marked Mirambeau.

Château de Sanse

33350 Sainte Radegonde
Gironde
Tel: +33 (0) 5 57 56 41 10
Fax: +33 (0) 5 57 56 41 29
contact@chateaudesanse.com
www.chateaudesanse.com

Rooms and rates
16 rooms
Double room for 2 people
per night from €110
Breakfast €12. Dinner from €26

Proprietor
Martin Edwards

Open
All year except February

Midway between the vineyards of St Emilion and the picture-book Dordogne, this 17th century château sits in five acres of meadows and woodland at the heart of Bordeaux wine country. It's stunning inside, with a light and contemporary feel that retains some of the building's grand original features (don't miss the magnificent fireplace in the dining room), while giving the place a distinctly modern twist. Outside, you can chill with a good book - or a glass of excellent local claret - by the heated pool or beneath the serene shade of the cedar trees. There's a helipad in the grounds if you choose to arrive in style.

C'est si bon!

Makes every Sanse to make this your base in the south west.

Bon repos Rooms are spacious and clutter-free, with off-white walls, Thai wickerwork chairs, nicely textured fabrics and immaculate bathrooms. Many have a private balcony or terrace where you can gaze over the Dordogne valley.

Bon appetit Expect all the flavours of the south west in chef Guillaume Depairé's inventive cooking, with menus featuring the château's own homegrown produce and herbs. Breakfast on fresh croissants and home-made jams in the new conservatory restaurant, where you can gaze out onto the lush valleys.

Bon temps You're spoiled for choice here. The medieval town of Saint Emilion is close by, while Bergerac and Bordeaux await exploration. The vineyards of Entre-Deux-Mers and Côtes de Castillon are right on the doorstep. Energetic types can go canoeing, horse riding or hot air ballooning - or head for Atlantic beaches 90 minutes away.

Bon voyage From Bordeaux: take the D936 to St Emilion and Castillon, then D17/18. Hotel is on D15E1 after Pujols.

La Maison Bord-eaux

113 rue Albert Barraud
33000 Bordeaux
Tel: +33 (0) 5 56 44 00 45
Fax: +33 (0) 5 56 44 17 31
contact@lamaisonbord-eaux.com
www.lamaisonbord-eaux.com

Rooms and rates
5 rooms
Double room for 2 people
per night from €150 to €200
Breakfast included

Proprietors
Brigitte Lurton & Jean-Marc Domingo

Open
Except 31 Jan and in August

This little place – bang in the midst of big-city Bordeaux – has bags of élan. Brigitte Lurton's new place fizzes with freshness and exuberant colour. Sherbert green, purple and plum red contrast with spick 'n' span polished wood floors, sleek lighting and contemporary art. Stay either in the three-storey main house, or in the 18th century stable block at the bottom of the garden. Rooms are named after the family's children and comforts are strictly 21st century, with internet access, satellite TV, and anti-UV windows. Brigitte and partner Jean-Marc Domingo have even designed some of their own furniture.

C'est si bon!

Plenty of zing in this slick little B&B. A place to get fresh!

Bon repos Clean-cut lines and freshly minted colours are partnered in the ultra-spacious and soundproofed bedrooms. King-size beds are dressed in Italian linens, fabrics are carefully chosen and bathrooms kitted out with robes, slippers and Hermès toiletries. Guests also have a supply of Italian coffee, Corsican mineral water and herbal teas.

Bon appetit Breakfast is a feast of Viennoiseries, season's fruit, yoghurt, cheese and freshly squeezed juices. You can eat your fill of local tapas at the cellar bar downstairs, stocked with the best of Bordeaux wines. There's also a seafood or cheese menu.

Bon temps The best of Bordeaux is at your feet. Check out the medieval and Gothic buildings behind impressive Place de Parlement, and stroll along the waterfront with its spruced-up 17th and 18th century houses. Bordeaux is synonymous with wine, so make time for some tastings at some of the region's 20,000 vineyards.

Bon voyage 25 minutes by taxi from Bordeaux Airport.

Les Sources de Caudalie

Chemin de Smith Haut-Lafitte
33650 Bordeaux-Martillac
Tel: +33 (0) 5 57 83 83 83
Fax: +33 (0) 5 57 83 83 84
reservations@sources-caudalie.com
www.sources-caudalie.com

Rooms and rates
40 rooms, 9 suites
Double room for 2 people
per night from €185 to €250
Breakfast from €18. Dinner from €32

General managers
Alice Cathiard and Jérôme Tourbier

Open
All year round

Bring together thermal springs, wine's life-enhancing properties and the art of haute cuisine and you have Les Sources de Caudalie, a place unlike any other. This evocative Bordeaux estate, built in 18th century timber in the style of a Gironde fishing village, complete with swan-filled lake and bucolic vineyards, is part luxury spa and part hotel. Guests leave refreshed and rejuvenated after a pampering at the sybaritic Spa de Vinotherapie, with its unique menu of feel-good treatments. Sitting beside the world-famous Château Smith Haut-Lafitte vineyard, this is a place where you'll be simply glowing from Bordeaux.

C'est si bon!

Serene, sexy, sensuous... unique wine-spa hotel where you'll have a vine time.

Bon repos Stay on the Isle aux Oiseaux and commune with nature in a cabin on stilts. Striking rooms are done out with wood floors and natural fabrics, while patios or decks invite the outside in. Marble bathrooms stocked with Caudalie goodies promise 24-hour indulgence.

Bon appetit Chef Franck Salein oversees cooking at La Grand'Vigne restaurant, and at La Table du Lavoir, a rustic auberge. Expect finesse and some delicate East/West fusion. The impeccable wine list features some 600 bins, including Bordeaux first-growths and the mythical 1878 Graves. Cigar smokers even have their own bar.

Bon temps There's no need to drag yourself away from the estate: get your fill here of blissful vine baths, wraps, facials and assorted spa treatments where grape extracts are used to revitalise and renew. Then swim, play tennis, pitch and putt, water-ski, and imbibe.

Bon voyage From Bordeaux Airport: take the A62 towards Toulouse, then Exit 1. Go to 4th roundabout and turn right.

Maison Arrokenia

15 rue Gardague
64200 Biarritz
Tel: +33 (0) 5 59 22 38 35
Fax: +33 (0) 5 59 26 48 47
maison.arrokenia@caramail.com
www.maisonarrokenia.com

Rooms and rates
4 suites
Suite for 2 people
per night from €120 to €180
Breakfast €10

Proprietor
Thérèse Gérard

Open
All year round

When interior decorator Thérèse Gérard took over this old family hotel that had fallen into wrack and ruin, the only things she kept intact were the staircase and the fig tree in the garden. Everything else in this supremely stylish four-suite Basque style property in the heart of Biarritz has been elegantly transformed behind signature wrought iron gates. Cool flagstoned floors, impeccably chosen furniture and objets d'art are set against deliciously understated soft and subtle colours ranging from dove grey and cream to prune and violet. A neat, freshly planted town garden is the nicest surprise, all minutes from the sea.

C'est si bon!

Suite serenity just yards from the Atlantic surf.

Bon repos Each of the four suites is named after the Basque region's prettiest villages. Ascain, with its canopied bed and carved wooden headboard, is a symphony of soft greys and gold. Arcangues, with its French doors leading to a sunny balcony, uses warmer shades of peach and burgundy, while Arbonne sports splashes of purple. Marble surrounds, sleek chrome fittings and thoughtful amenities make bathrooms a treat.

Bon appetit Breakfast is served on the patio in warm weather, and Thérèse is happy to make recommendations for dinners out nearby. With the Atlantic just minutes away, freshly-caught fish is always on the menu du jour.

Bon temps Biarritz is an outdoor holiday playground, so hit the surf on those famous beaches or swing a club on fairways set against a backdrop of the Pyrenees. Treat yourself to some pampering at the Marine Thalassotherapy Spa or get in the saddle at the equestrian centre.

Bon voyage 10 mins by taxi from TGV station and airport.

Maison Garnier

29 rue Gambetta
64200 Biarritz
Tel: +33 (0) 5 59 01 60 70
Fax: +33 (0) 5 59 01 60 80
maison-garnier@hotel-biarritz.com
www.hotel-biarritz.com

Rooms and rates
7 rooms
Double room for 2 people
per night from €80 to €120
Breakfast €9

Proprietor
Yves Gelot

Open
All year round

Forget the big beachfront palaces of this famous Atlantic resort: instead, seek out this intimate little corner house, quietly situated uphill just five minutes from the ocean's tumbling waves. Rescued from dereliction and charmingly renovated, Maison Garnier (named after the previous owner) is bright, light and stylish, with a mix of quirky, quality modern and 30s furniture. The result is highly appealing, and the cosy fireplace lounge downstairs is the centre of conviviality. New owner Yves Gelot and his wife are the friendliest hosts. Those in the know find its sophisticated simplicity quite irresistible - not to mention great value.

C'est si bon!

One of Biarritz's little secrets - shhh, don't tell...

Bon repos Spacious rooms display soft tobacco, cream and ebony tints. That, and the quiet location, encourage sound sleep - unless guests are in the room under the rafters reserved for lovers and honeymooners (say no more). Spotless baths have large retro-style showers.

Bon appetit Trouble's taken with petit déjeuner - expect to wake up to freshly squeezed Basque orange juice and a selection of healthy cereals, yoghurts, melting croissants and brioches, and strong coffee (perfect fuel for surfing). Yves will point you towards some of the town's excellent fish restaurants for dinner.

Bon temps Biarritz is a real beach-lover's resort where surfers can pursue their passion year-round. Hydrangea-decked streets are crammed with bijou stores, there's a slick casino, and summer sees festivals galore. Play golf against ocean or Pyrenees mountain backdrops or bliss out in five thalassotherapy centres.

Bon voyage 10 minutes by taxi from TGV station.

La ferme de Bassilour

Rue Burruntz
64210 Bidart
Tel: +33 (0) 5 59 41 90 85
Fax: +33 (0) 5 59 41 87 62
bassilour@gsc.fr
www.domainedebassilour.com

Rooms and rates
10 rooms
Double room for 2 people
per night from €80 to €150
Breakfast €10

Proprietor
Charlotte Vachet

Open
All year round

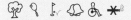

Take a 17th century farmhouse and hot up its interiors with a dash of Scandinavian design flair and you have Ferme de Bassilour, tucked on the edge of a tranquil Basque village. This rustic 17th century chambre d'hôte forms part of the Domaine de Bassilour, with its pretty gardens and Second Empire mansion. Owner Charlotte Vachet runs the ferme and her fiefdom with some style; her Swedish background reveals itself in Nordic touches throughout. Outside, guests have tables on the terrace for relaxation, rural views of the Pyrenees on one side and the Atlantic ocean minutes away on the other. A brilliant find.

C'est si bon!

Great style, great value and lashings of rural peace.

Bon repos The fabric of the building has been used to great effect here: exposed stonework, bricks and rafters are set off by blond woods, polished floors, crisp linens and cool off-whites. Swish lighting and the latest luxury bathroom fittings (we loved the shower tiled entirely with pebbles) complete the look.

Bon appetit Breakfast – deliciously done with home-made breads and jams – is served in the striking wood-beamed lounge, with its old flagstone floor and open fireplace. Charlotte has the gen on a number of good restaurants within easy driving distance.

Bon temps Biarritz and its fabulous beaches are just a few miles away. A tennis court and horses are right in the grounds, and five golf courses lie within easy reach. Walking trails and pretty Basque countryside await discovery close by.

Bon voyage From Biarritz: Take the A63 or N10 south. Turn left at Bidart.

Les frères Ibarboure

Chemin de Ttaliénèa
64210 Guéthary
Tel: +33 (0) 5 59 47 58 30
Fax: +33 (0) 5 59 54 75 65
contact@freresibarboure.com
www.freresibarboure.com

Rooms and rates
8 rooms
Double room for 2 people
per night from €130 to €230
Breakfast €13. Dinner from €40

Proprietors
Philippe and Martin Ibarboure

Open
Except 15 Nov - 7 Dec and 4-20 Jan

With fashionable Biarritz just a short drive away, the restaurant and hotel of Les Frères Ibarboure enjoys all its associated elegance and glamour while sitting serenely in a village setting. Bordered by flowers and sweeping pine forests on the upper slopes of Guéthary, and just minutes from the sea, it's an inviting retreat with plenty of Basque allure. Brothers Philippe (the chef), Martin (the patissier) and their wives have been running this little gastronomic gem for the past 15 years. It has a nicely intimate feel, and comforts are on a par with the terrific cuisine. The owners are charmers.

C'est si bon!

Where a tiny Arcadia
meets Basque country.

Bon repos Each of the evocatively named eight bedrooms (choose between Moonlight, Atlantic Reflections and Forest Edge) opens on to its own terrace overlooking the pool or forest. Tasteful and eclectic furnishings are big on comfort, while bathrooms are the business.

Bon appetit Restaurateurs Philippe and Martin are clearly passionate about food. Resolutely Basque, their cuisine du terroir harnesses the best of the region's game and fresh produce, not to mention fresh-landed ocean catches. Dine in the contemporary Rotonde room, the charming La Chapelle or La Veranda, with its flower-decked terrace.

Bon temps Follow paths of lush greenery down towards the Atlantic for quiet or sporting pleasures. The surfing beaches of Biarritz and the nightlife of Saint-Jean-de-Luz are close by, while the Pyrenees provide a stunning mountain backdrop for further discovery.

Bon voyage From Biarritz: take the A63 or N10 south. The hotel is signed from the main road at Guéthary.

Villa Catarie

Avenue du Général de Gaulle
64210 Guéthary
Tel: +33 (0) 5 59 47 59 00
Fax: +33 (0) 5 59 47 59 02
info@villa-catarie.com
www.villa-catarie.com

Rooms and rates
16 rooms
Double room for 2 people
per night from €120 to €165
Breakfast €11

Proprietor
Peggy Alday

Open
December – October

Sitting pretty in the village of Guéthary, between the last crest of the Pyrenees and the Atlantic Ocean, Villa Catarie is a nest for diehard romantics. With its painted shutters and balconies (ideal for catching rays and Atlantic sea breezes) this 18th century Basque house glows with soft-focus colour and comforts. Stylishly done out in kitten-soft creams, peach and pastels, it enjoys a delightful small terrace garden – perfect for sipping a glass of local Txakoli wine at dusk – and a pool. Its village location away from the bustle of nearby Biarritz adds to its sense of relaxed seclusion. A winner in the charm stakes.

C'est si bon!

A place to Basque in the pleasures of this gorgeous corner of France.

Bon repos Owner Peggy Alday – film-maker turned hotel owner – is the stylish hand behind the decor. Lovers are cocooned in a symphony of pastel greys, pearly pinks and soft whites. Well soundproofed rooms feature painted antiques, mood lighting and quality fabrics. The effect is supremely restful. Great bathrooms, too.

Bon appetit Delicious breakfasts include regional delicacies, nicely served. Good restaurants where local specialities might include Bayonne hams, stuffed peppers, Biscayne salt cod and wood pigeon abound.

Bon temps The hotel's less than 500 metres from long sandy beaches, coves and cliff walks. At certain points along the shoreline Atlantic breakers roll in: grab a board, surf's up. There are numerous 18-hole golf courses nearby, and fashionable Biarritz, not far away, hosts any number of cultural festivals.

Bon voyage From Biarritz: Take the A63 or N10 south. The hotel is signed after the Guéthary turn-off.

le Parc Victoria

5 rue Cépé
64500 Saint Jean-de-Luz
Tel: +33 (0) 5 59 26 78 78
Fax: +33 (0) 5 59 26 78 08
parcvictoria@relaischateaux.com
www.parcvictoria.com

Rooms and rates
9 rooms, 8 suites
Double room for 2 people
per night from €155 to €257
Breakfast €15. Dinner from €36

Proprietor
Roger Larralde

Open
15 March - 15 November

Rather lovely, this foamy-white Victorian mansion in the old port of Saint Jean-de-Luz in the heart of Pays Basque, is just a short hop from the Spanish border. The two owners rescued it ten years ago, transforming the interior into twin temples of Art Deco and Nouveau. Stylishly assembled objets d'art, statuary, furniture and lighting impart an expensive fin-de-siècle atmosphere. Outside it's no less striking; lush and peaceful parkland, terraces with exotic plantings and a seductive summerhouse and pool induce guests to bask all day long. 'Ongi Etorri' ('welcome' in Basque lingo) carries conviction from owners and staff.

C'est si bon!

A perfect place to Parc yourselves in Pays Basque.

Bon repos Flair and indulgence has gone into designing the 17 rooms, with their broadly Art Deco theme. The result is idiosyncratic and characterful (comfy besides). Large marble baths show care, and many have jacuzzis.

Bon appetit Chef Eric Jorge's inspired regional à la carte and set menus maintain delectable consistency whether enjoyed poolside, in the winter-garden conservatory or in the plush Les Lierres dining room. His signature dishes include poêlée de langoustine au cidre basque; tournedos de veau au chorizo; and delicious tarte aux poires pochées.

Bon temps Options? Plentiful. The pool scene sizzles in summer, and there are beach frolics and nautical sports just five minutes away. Nearby are two golf courses and indoor/outdoor tennis courts; riding and kayaking; thalasso-therapy for tired muscles and four museums to engage brain cells. You could also take a 4x4 up into the hills.

Bon voyage From Biarritz: exit from the A63 at Saint Jean-de-Luz nord and turn right after the 4th traffic lights.

La Devinière

5 rue Loquin
64500 Saint-Jean-de-Luz
Tel: +33 (0) 5 59 26 05 51
Fax: +33 (0) 5 59 51 26 38
la.deviniere.64@wanadoo.fr
www.hotel-la-deviniere.com

Rooms and rates
10 rooms
Double room for 2 people
per night from €110 to €150
Breakfast €10

Proprietors
Bernard and Marie-France Carrère

Open
All year round

What delights lurk down the aimiable side streets of buzzy Saint-Jean-de-Luz? Well, there's La Devinière for a start. This house, with its unmistakable Basque exterior, was home to Bernard and Marie-France Carrère until they converted it into a small hotel. Not surprisingly, it retains all the spirit of a loved and lived-in home: the lounge overflows with books and a medley of ornaments; walls are lined with their daughter's paintings (rather good); there's a fireplace for cold evenings and the prettiest little garden for enjoying warm ones. A 19th century Beckstein grand takes centre stage for the hotel's regular musical soirées.

C'est si bon!

Pretty Basque townhouse that resonates with country charm.

Bon repos Guests could find themselves sleeping in a four-poster or antique wooden Basque bed. Rooms are individually decorated with antiques, books and knick-knacks; as personable as you might find in the country home of a stylish friend.

Bon appetit Breakfast on home-made breads and jams in your room or in the rustic salle à manger. There's also a choice of 30 different teas, plus chocolate. In fine weather, soak up the rays in the little garden.

Bon temps You're just yards from the resort's sweep of golden sands, so make the most of beach life and nautical sports. Mosy around the picturesque old port; play golf (there are nine courses nearby), and peep into the church of Saint Jean-Baptiste where Louis XIV married the Spanish Infanta in 1660. Feeling adventurous? Slip across the border to Bilbao to check out the Guggenheim Museum.

Bon voyage 30 mins from Biarritz by frequent train or bus; or 25 mins by car on the N10.

The Central valleys:
The Auvergne, Dordogne, Tarn and Lot

Aller for la vie gourmande
Manger foie gras and truffles – the region's darkest delight
Santé! Saussignac and sweet Monzabillac

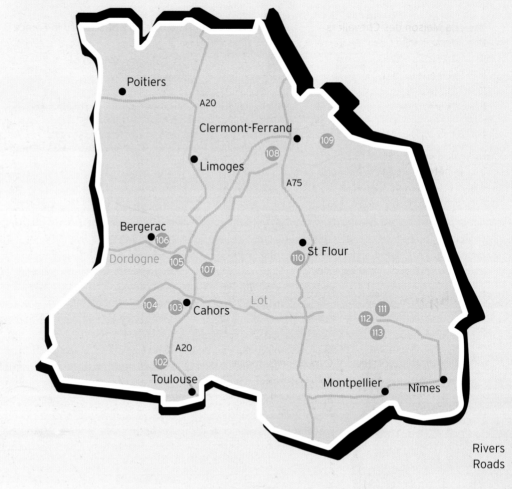

Pages 102 – 113

Why?

There's a stunning diversity of scenery in France's heartland – from the clifftop châteaux of the Dordogne to the craggy gorges of the Lot and Tarn valleys, the unspoiled wilderness of the Cévennes and the volcanic cones and craters of the Auvergne. A naturalist's paradise, this is also truffle country – and a place to shop at wonderful outdoor markets piled high with cheeses, local delicacies and oven-fresh breads.

So why not...♥

- Paddle off in a canoe for two on the Lot and Dordogne rivers
- Clamber up the steep-sided Aveyron gorges
- Follow in the footsteps of Cyrano de Bergerac (you'll see his statue in Bergerac town)
- See the celebrated Lascaux cave paintings
- Wander through the streets of medieval Uzès

La Maison des Chevaliers

Place de la Mairie
82700 Escatalens
Tel: +33 (0) 5 63 68 71 23
Fax: +33 (0) 5 63 30 25 90
claude.choux@wanadoo.fr
www.maisondeschevaliers.com

Rooms and rates
1 room, 3 suites
Double room for 2 people
per night from €65
Breakfast included. Dinner from €20

Proprietors
Claude and Claudine Choux

Open
All year round

Sitting right next to the village church, this solid 18th century residence sits in rural resplendence close to the river Garonne midway between the Lot and the Tarn valleys. Creeper-covered red brick walls and white painted shutters lend it an air that's both lordly and country-comfy. Rooms overlook a serene and sunny courtyard dotted with wrought iron tables and chairs and inside, guests practically have the run of the place. There's a library crammed with books, a pool beckoning through the garden trees, and even a guest kitchen in the old wine cellars in case you fancy playing chef for the night...

C'est si bon!

Award-winning maison d'hôtes with style, charm and conviviality.

Bon repos Rooms big enough to play hide-and-seek in have a touch of theatricality, with the odd trompe l'oeil or painted fresco. Painted cupboards, carved armoires, old hearths and splashes of extrovert colour add style. Roméo et Juliette has a vast faux-marble bathroom, while a magnificent staircase opens into the Suites des Chevaliers.

Bon appetit Say no more – owner Claudine Choux, who used to run her own restaurants in Portugal, is a Cordon Bleu chef whose regional French cooking hits the spot. Guests dine in the leafy courtyard beneath the shade of the chestnut tree in fine weather.

Bon temps This is countryside for exploring. You can paddle off in your own canoe, play tennis, ride and fish nearby, or head off for the Tarn gorges. Toulouse, with its contemporary art museum and Cité d'Espace science park, is also within striking distance. Feeling idle? Simply lounge in a hammock by the pool.

Bon voyage From Toulouse: take the N20 and N113.

Domaine de Saint Géry

46800 Lascabanes
Tel: +33 (0) 5 65 31 82 51
Fax: +33 (0) 5 65 22 92 89
infos@saint-gery.com
www.saint-gery.com

Rooms and rates
4 rooms, 1 suite
Double room per person
per night from €158 to €264
Breakfast and dinner included

Proprietors
Pascale and Patrick Duler

Open
Mid May – October

Couples who want to escape the crowds (and who love to eat well) should check out this little world: a collection of ancient buildings in local calcaire stone bordered by fragrant lemon and fig trees and framed by hilly Quercy forests. This has been Patrick and Pascale Duler's labour of love for the last 20 years; the couple successfully run an auberge and reputable restaurant alongside a working farm of 60 hectares producing some famed staples of haute cuisine. The environment created exudes stylish calm within and without, and a tranquil pool completes the Duler domain.

C'est si bon!

Foodies should definitely register their interest at this Domaine.

Bon repos Tucked high beneath beamed eaves with wood or stone floors, rooms come with vaulted brickwork interiors, rustic antiques and splendid bathrooms. Guests can beat a path to the pool from private terraces with garden views.

Bon appetit Patrick's modern cooking is epicurean. Dishes come scented with farm truffles (try the carpaccio de magret), while foie gras and confit are specialities. The potager provides organic herbs and vegetables, and Pascale's desserts are a treat. Diners gather around a communal table, and there's terrace eating in summer.

Bon temps Woodland running trails, a fitness room and, of course, the pool (heated), should keep you out of trouble. Nearby, venerable old towns and gorgeous Lot countryside collude here: visit Cahors, historic St. Cirq Lapopie and Rocamadour. Play golf, canoe and waterski. Markets and festivals proliferate from summer to autumn.

Bon voyage From Toulouse: take the N20 via Montauban. Turn on to D653 and turn left for Lascabanes.

Château Lalande

47140 Saint-Sylvestre-sur-Lot
Périgord
Tel: +33 (0) 5 53 36 15 15
Fax: +33 (0) 5 53 36 15 16
chateau.lalande@wanadoo.fr
www.chateau-lalande.com

Rooms and rates
18 rooms, 4 suites
Double room for 2 people
per night from €145 to €350
Breakfast €15. Dinner from €37

Director
Yves Prenat

Open
All year round

Seen one château, seen them all? Well, this one is rather spiffy. Approached through scenic parkland (and with its own helipad) Château Lalande boasts an elegant and towered 18th century frontage. The magnificent pool and spa complex, surrounded by a villa-style terrace, triumphal stone arches and giant terracotta pots, almost looks like part of the Roman empire. Inside, richly appointed salons display chandeliers and period furniture while modern pieces fit in gracefully. Subtle evening floodlighting enhances the patrician atmosphere, imbuing the château with a sumptuous fairytale glow.

C'est si bon!

Land your helicopter at Lalande, then lap up luxurious spa comforts.

Bon repos There's no lack of lavish nocturnal comforts, whether you choose a suite, deluxe or poolside room. Aside from views of the grounds or light dancing off the water, guests can enjoy pleasing decor and antiques, feathersoft beds and sophisticated bathrooms.

Bon appetit Chef Philippe Mourot serves dishes to re-awaken the palate in two pretty restaurants (one classic, one offering lighter fare) alongside fine regional wines. His four imaginative menus – which include Dégustation and Surprise du Château – taste as terrific as they sound.

Bon temps What a grand Lot: there's the Lot valley itself, with medieval Penne d'Agenais' impressive basilica; the eighth century Bastide de Monflanquin; and picturesque Villeneuve-sur-Lot. Lots of energy? There's tennis, golf, water skiing and paragliding. Lots of spoiling? Try some of those spa treatments.

Bon voyage From Bordeaux: leave the A62 at Exit 6 for Aiguillon, then join D911 to Villeneuve and St Sylvestre.

La ferme Lamy

24220 Meyrals
Tel: +33 (0) 5 53 29 62 46
Fax: +33 (0) 5 53 59 61 41
ferme-lamy@wanadoo.fr
www.ferme-lamy.com

Rooms and rates
12 rooms
Double room for 2 people
per night from €95 to €200
Breakfast €10-15

Proprietors
Nelly and Michel Bougon

Open
All year round

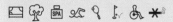

This 17th century farmhouse has been converted into a supremely comfortable hotel with all the trimmings – without losing its air of rural simplicity. Spacious, comfortable and elegantly furnished rooms are framed by sturdy wooden beams, while outside, majestic walnut trees surround a swimming pool that's pure Florida. The garden is full of colours and scents that vary with the seasons – lime flowers, honeysuckle and roses – while there's more than a hint of bonne cuisine coming from the kitchen. Nothing is too much trouble for proprietors Nelly and Michel Bougon, in this rustic idyll overlooking rolling green pastures.

C'est si bon!

All rustic charm here: flower-filled gardens and farmhouse-fresh cooking.

Bon repos There's something special about each of the 12 rooms: one is a sprawling 40 sq m, easily large enough to swing a cat or tame a tiger. Another has its own outside staircase for moonlit trysts under the stars. And there's one with a jacuzzi for two.

Bon appetit Follow your nose to the kitchen, where Nelly bakes old-fashioned butter brioches and crusty walnut bread. These treats, and home-made jams, make their way to the breakfast table on the shady terrace or by the pool. This is truffle country, so your dishes could be studded with black gold when you dine out...

Bon temps If history turns you on, you'll love exploring the region's medieval villages, archaeological sites and prehistoric dwellings – so get in touch with your inner caveman. The lovely Dordogne is just a short drive away, and there's ample scope for tennis, golf and canoeing.

Bon voyage From Bordeaux: join A89 towards Perigueux; take N89/D47 to Les Eyzies, then C3 to Meyrals.

Château Lespinassat

24100 Bergerac
Tel: +33 (0) 5 53 74 84 11
Fax: +33 (0) 5 53 74 83 30
chateaulespinassat@wanadoo.fr
www.chateaulespinassat.com

Rooms and rates
1 room, 2 suites
Double room/suite for 2 people
per night from €120 to €290
Breakfast included.
Dinner from €30-40

Proprietors
Marion Schildhorn & Christian Calès

Open
All year round

As there are only three rooms and suites at 18th century Château Lespinassat, guests have it almost to themselves. This newly renovated historic building is quite something: apart from terrace and moat, there are 12 acres of scenic parkland dotted with cedars, cypress and lime trees and, what's more, an ornamental lake where kingfishers and cormorants swoop. Inside, various panelled or fabric-lined salons with decorative ceilings, period furniture and paintings delight the eye. Lovers can take advantage of its privacy to wander the gardens, dip in the pool, sip champagne and sneak kisses unseen.

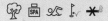

C'est si bon!

Blissful Bergerac château in which to indulge in a little folie de grandeur.

Bon repos Flowers, fruit and nuts, and a complimentary drink await arriving guests, and the two sumptuous suites have fireplaces. Isaure de Saint-Aignan is spaciously elegant à la Louis XV, with jacuzzi and courtyard access, while the others offer their own comforts.

Bon appetit It's just like having your own chef here: after delicious home-made breakfast treats guests can discuss with the owners their particular fancy for dinner. Meals with outstanding wines are served in the salon, glowing with chandeliers, fire and candlelight.

Bon temps Right on hand are a pool and pretty gardens; on form nearby are three golf courses; on tap are Bordeaux, Bergerac and Saint-Emilion vineyards. The Dordogne valley, splendiferous Lanquais and Beynac châteaux, stalactite caves, and Les Eyzies, France's prehistoric capital, are the icing on top.

Bon voyage From the centre of Bergerac, take the N1 towards Saint-Christophe and Agen.

Château de la Treyne

46200 Lacave, Lot
Tel: +33 (0) 5 65 27 60 60
Fax: +33 (0) 5 65 27 60 70
contact@chateaudelatreyne.com
www.chateaudelatreyne.com

Rooms and rates
14 rooms, 2 suites
Double room for 2 people
per night from €180 to €480
Breakfast €18. Dinner from €72

Proprietors
Michèle and Philippe Gombert

Open
Except 15 Nov - 21 Dec
and 6 Jan - 22 March

Here's a château that's the stuff of dreams: the sort of place where you could happily lock yourselves in the tower and throw away the keys. Perched on a cliffy hilltop overlooking the Dordogne and dating back to the 14th century, Château de la Treyne is steeped in history and brimming with romance, from its creamy stone turrets and mullioned windows to its hand-carved four-posters. Beyond the doors, a 300-acre domain of private woodland stretches away, inviting hand-in-hand moonlit strolls. Nouba, the castle's friendly Labrador, is happy to act as chaperone for couples in danger of getting carried away with it all.

C'est si bon!

Just the place for a divine Dordogne dalliance.

Bon repos Lavish bedrooms, many with rich wallcoverings, Louis XIII furniture and bathtubs for two, are just the place to be led into temptation. Bed down in the 14th century tower, with its criss-cross rafters and peek-a-boo views, or be comrades in arms in the Henry IV bedroom. One room has its own private terrace overlooking the Dordogne.

Bon appetit Breakfast beneath 100-year-old cedars, float down the river with a gourmet picnic or dine on the gorgeous river terrace at night. Chef Stéphane Andrieux's signature dishes include foie gras frais de canard served with fig chutney, nuts and Monbazillac jelly.

Bon temps Walk in the woods, warm up on the tennis court or cool down in the pool. If you're not already on a high, you could even take off in a hot-air balloon or helicopter from the front lawns. Explore Sarlat, Beynac and La Roque Gageac, and the cave paintings at Lascaux.

Bon voyage From Toulouse: take the A20 via Cahors to Exit 55 (Souillac sud) and the D43 towards Pinsac/Lacave.

La Vigie

63320 Chadeleuf
Tel: +33 (0) 4 73 96 90 87
Fax: +33 (0) 4 73 96 92 76
pineauveronique@wanadoo.fr
perso.wanadoo.fr/chadeleuf.lavigie/

Rooms and rates
2 rooms
Double room for 2 people
per night from €55 to €65
Breakfast included. Dinner €18

Proprietors
Véronique and Denis Pineau

Open
All year round

Right at the foot of the Auvergne's stunning Parc des Volcans – a place like no other in Europe – this bijou little maison d'hôte offers the perfect place to tarry awhile. Neglected for 50 years, La Vigie now echoes to the cheerful sounds of family life once more, thanks to the energy and enthusiasm of owners Véronique and Denis Pineau. They have chased away the cobwebs and created a little gem of a place in this welcoming village house with its blue-painted shutters and tall chimneys. With just two guestrooms and an inviting book-lined lounge, booking ahead is de rigueur.

C'est si bon!

Village charmer in the heart of volcano country.

Bon repos Centrepiece of the suite-sized Ivory room is an extravagant four-poster bed voluptuously draped in white muslin tied back with cords. Distress-painted wooden beams, white rugs, soft lighting and a fireplace make it a boudoir worth lingering in.

Bon appetit This is a place for healthy living, with delicious wholemeal breads and home-made jams for breakfast. Dinner is served to order twice a week, when you can join fellow guests or your convivial hosts at the table. Expect delicious Auvergne cuisine with a veggie and organic slant.

Bon temps Idle away the day at the property's terraced pool, or head for the wild beauty of the volcano park, with its lakes, craters, caves and volcanic cones. You can discover its many wonders on foot, on cycles, on horseback or from the air, in a light aircraft or paraglider. Rare birds abound, and the mountain-fresh air alone is a tonic.

Bon voyage From Clermond Ferrand: take the A75 and leave at Exit 9 for Chadeleuf. Turn left after the Mairie.

Château de Codignat

Bort l'Etang
63190 LEZOUX
Tel: +33 (0) 4 73 68 43 03
Fax: +33 (0) 4 73 68 93 54
codignat@relaischateaux.com
www.codignat.com

Rooms and rates
15 rooms, 5 suites
Double room for 2 people
per night from €360 to €515
Breakfast included. Dinner from €50

General manager
Denis Lesage

Open
19 March – 1 November

Fancy lording it in a 15th century feudal château surrounded by the lakes, forests and volcanic hills of the Auvergne? Set in its own 37,000 acres, this turreted castle still possesses the solid stone floors and walls, massive chimney pieces and pediments of yore. Add to that sumptuous soft furnishings, choice antiques and modern comforts and you have the best of both worlds. Historic atmosphere really does seem to ooze from those walls. Where in the past the occupants donned armour and rode off to war, today's pace is more leisurely: a swim in the pool, drinks in the shady arbour, walks between ancient oaks.

C'est si bon!

What views! This château looks towards the volcanoes of Auvergne (eruptions not expected).

Bon repos Spacious rooms, some with four-posters, are decorated in Haute Epoque style with gilded or Romanesque furniture, tapestries, needlepoint cushions and extravagant draperies. Bathrooms are marbled, and in another stylistic union, some have murals and jacuzzis.

Bon appetit Dreamy dining here: tables are draped with delicate local lace, lit by candles and laid with gold-edged plates and crystal goblets. Firelight flickers in the hearth, while a Michelin-starred menu of local and national cuisine leaves an even warmer glow.

Bon temps Take advantage of the varied landscape: ride a helicopter over volcanoes; follow the châteaux and fortress trail; saddle up for plains and valleys; go boating or take the spa waters; tour Vulcania theme park; visit museums celebrating the best of Romanesque art.

Bon voyage From Clermont-Ferrand: take the motorway towards Lyon, exit at Lezoux, head for the town centre and follow the Courpière Road, towards Bort-l'Etang.

Château de Varillettes

15100 St Georges
Tel: +33 (0) 4 71 60 45 05
Fax: +33 (0) 4 71 60 34 27
varillettes@leshotelsparticuliers.com
www.chateaudevarillettes.com

Rooms and rates
11 rooms, 2 apartments
Double room for 2 people
per night from €107 to €200
Breakfast €12. Dinner from €21-42

Proprietors
Les Hôtels Particuliers - Groupe Savry
Manager: Nelly Mestre

Open
April - October

The scent of sage, hyssop and lavender wafts over guests strolling around the herb garden which abuts this former 15th century keep. True to its military past, the château stands guard in a valley bordered by the fields and woods facing the Auvergne's Margaride hills. Following centuries as the country home of various dignitaries, it is now one of Philippe Savry's collection of courtly châteaux and has been given a much-deserved makeover. The glow of old floors, carved armoires and imposing brick hearths complements a royal colour palette of plum reds, yellows and blues. Down in the woods, there's another delight: a tiny hermitage.

C'est si bon!

Historic castle keep you'd be happy to stay in for keeps.

Bon repos Creature comforts are far removed from those of yore. Bedrooms strike a more contemporary note, with comfortable beds, elegant soft furnishings, fabric-lined walls and nicely appointed bathrooms.

Bon appetit Today's diners eat by candlelight beneath the vaulted stone arches of the dining room, where a fire blazes on cooler nights. Look forward to feasting on a menu du terroir using the region's best: that might mean locally cured meats, puy lentils and Cantal cheeses.

Bon temps After strolling through the medieval gardens, it's an easy stretch for tennis, riding or walks through moorland and valleys crossed by streams (tried canoeing yet?). Saint-Flour, known as the City of Bishops, has a striking Gothic cathedral with France's only black Christ. Hot spas spring eternal in Chaudes-Aigues.

Bon voyage From Clermont-Ferrand, take the A75 south and turn off at exit 29 (D926) towards Saint-Flour. Follow signs to the left for Varillettes.

Château de Saint-Maximin

Rue du Château
30700 St Maximin
Tel: +33 (0) 4 66 03 44 16
Fax: +33 (0) 4 66 03 42 98
info@chateaustmaximin.com
www.chateaustmaximin.com

Rooms and rates
4 rooms, 2 suites
Double room/suite for 2 people
per night from €145 to €320
Breakfast included. Dinner from €42

Director
Jean-Marc Perry

Open
All year except February

In the heart of French Tuscany, this noble château positively oozes history. Its oldest parts date back to the 12th century, since when it has lost none of its eclecticism and grace. A favourite haunt of the great neo-classical playwright Jean Racine, Saint Maximin retains a sense of heady drama even today – although the only tragedy you'll sense is that you can't stay forever. The cool golden stone, shady courtyard and distant sound of church bells make for an atmospheric setting, showcasing the owner's fabulous collection of stylish 1930s art and artefacts. Outside, classical statues and arches adorn the pool terrace and garden.

C'est si bon!

Serene, civilised, and chic: this place has sumptuous style.

Bon repos The six lavishly sized suites are named after Racine's heroines and individually decorated, so you can match your boudoir to your mood: choose minimalist stone and monochrome in classy Andromaque; warm shades of ochre and saffron in Iphigénie; deepest wine red in Phaedre. Bathrooms are decorated to perfection.

Bon appetit Breakfast outside under the jasmine arbour, gazing across at groves of silvery olive trees and the rooftops of the village, will set you up for the day. The hotel's cellar restaurant (open Wednesday to Sunday), serves local specialities in the evening.

Bon temps There's a heated outdoor pool, a gym and Turkish bath (yes, you can have it all to yourselves). Golf, mountain biking, riding, kayaking and the walking trails of the Cévennes beckon if you can bear to leave the seclusion of your suite.

Bon voyage From Avignon: take the N100, D19and D981 via Remoulins and Pont du Gard. Village is on the right.

Hostellerie le Castellas

Grand'Rue
30210 Collias
Tel: +33 (0) 4 66 22 88 88
Fax: +33 (0) 4 66 22 84 28
lecastellas@wanadoo.fr
www.lecastellas.com

Rooms and rates
15 rooms, 2 suites
Double room for 2 people
per night from €72 to €187
Breakfast €15. Dinner from €42

Proprietors
Chantal and Raymond Aparis

Open
All year except 2 Jan - 12 Feb

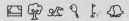

A number of centuries-old pale stone and green-shuttered buildings form this delightful enclave framed by tall cypress and palm trees. Little passageways nudge shady nooks and crannies where pots overflow with lavender and geraniums; here and there are tiny roof terraces and trellised balconies with tumbling greenery, while a small stairway leads to a hidden pool that captures the sun all day. Overlooking the garden, the bar is just the place for a glass of chilled pastis. Owners Chantal and Raymond Aparis and their daughter Aurélie radiate charm and efficiency in this dreamy domain.

C'est si bon!

The personification of provençal charm - enough to get pulses racing.

Bon repos Rooms are individualistic, so what takes your fancy? Something that stylishly recalls the arts, Nouveau or Deco; exotic hints of Egypt; or provençal white-washed walls, terracotta floors and polished beams? Among bathrooms of character is one with a floor made entirely from pebbles (strangely comfortable underfoot).

Bon appetit A pretty vaulted dining room decorated in pastels leads onto a charmingly atmospheric and ivy-clad terrace. Whether it's under sunny skies for petit déjeuner or in candlelight on balmy evenings, there's no resisting chef Jerome Nutile's tempting cuisine.

Bon temps The village is all stone houses and narrow winding streets; just the place to ramble. Not far is the magnificent viaduct crossing the Gordon gorge with rivers safe for canoeing, and banks for picnicking. Take trips further afield to medieval Uzès or Avignon.

Bon voyage From the A9, exit at Remoulins on D981 for Uzès, then join D12 to Collias. Follow signs in village.

Château d'Arpaillargues

Arpaillargues, 30700 Uzès
Tel: +33 (0) 4 66 22 14 48
Fax: +33 (0) 4 66 22 56 10
arpaillargues@leshotelsparticuliers.com
www.leshotelsparticuliers.com

Rooms and rates
27 rooms, 2 apartments
Double room for 2 people
per night from €69 to €235
Breakfast €12. Dinner €45-60

Proprietors
Les Hôtels Particuliers - Groupe Savry
Manager: Benjamin Savry

Open
1 April - 1 November

The foot-thick stone walls of this handsome Tuscan-style villa suggest a history stretching back further than its 18th century appearance. The patina of age is everywhere here, and the feel is not so much that of a hotel than of a comfy aristocratic home. Possessed of some style, the château is furnished with an eye for interesting antiques. Some of these remain from its time as home to the Comtesse d'Agoult, lover of Franz Liszt, and mother of Cosima Wagner. The atmosphere is such that you can easily imagine an étude or two floating airily through its salons bathed in provençal light. Its location near Uzès is a plus, too.

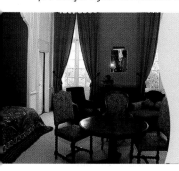

C'est si bon!

Add yourself to the guest liszt - the composer famously consorted here.

Bon repos Guests can bed down in one of 28 classily decorated rooms and suites, or choose the intimacy of two village houses. All enjoy a common theme: tall ceilings, alluring views and draped full-length windows offering that characteristic southern light. Some bathrooms have allegorical murals.

Bon appetit On balmy nights the courtyard terrace, with its floodlit blonde stonework and candlelit tables, really comes into its own. Not that the vaulted dining rooms feel in the least second best: as an American perusing the menu of choice provençal delicacies opined: 'What's not to like?'

Bon temps The pool is a real sun spot, ideal for lovers dipping or lazing. There's tennis or golf too, and you could aim higher with a balloon flight. The nearby hilltop town of Uzès, all golden-stone Renaissance facades with its own medieval fortress and gardens, is a gem.

Bon voyage From Nîmes: take the D979 to Uzès. Turn left on to the D982 to Arpaillargues and look for signs.

Burgundy & beyond:
From vintage Burgundy to the Alps

Aller for foodie France
Manger bouef bourguignon, escargots, coq au vin
Santé! Côtes de Beaune, Puligny-Montrachet

A 31
Dijon
Beaune
A39
A6
118
Macon
Geneva
119
Chamonix
117
116
120
Lyon
Annecy
St Etienne
A41
Grenoble
A7
Briançon
121
Valence

Rivers
Roads

Pages 116 – 121

Why?

Burgundy's celebrated gastronomy and legendary wine towns make it heaven for bon vivants. Good living has become an art form here, and the region's sublime food and wine is rivalled only by its art and historic treasures. Scenery, too, is a trump card where the Burgundian countryside melts into the chocolate-box Alpine scenery of Haute-Savoie - all lakes, forest and jagged peaks clad in snow.

So why not...♥

- Visit the famous vineyards of Beaune and Puligny-Montrachet
- Go mountain walking in matchless Alpine surroundings
- Get on the piste with the crunch of snow in winter
- See Mont Blanc the easy way - from a scenic cable car ride
- Share a raclette - gooey melted cheese eaten with potatoes and ham

Cour des Loges

2-8 rue de Bœuf
69005 Lyon
Tel: +33 (0) 4 72 77 44 44
Fax: +33 (0) 4 72 40 93 61
contact@courdesloges.com
www.c-h-m.com

Rooms and rates
62 rooms
Double room for 2 people
per night from €230 to €370
Breakfast €22. Dinner from €55

General manager
Jocelyne Sibuet

Open
All year round

Take four magnificent Italian Renaissance buildings in Lyon's old town. Artfully link them in such a way that the massive stone framework is faithfully preserved, then play unexpected tricks with the ancient interior by overlaying history with a decisively contemporary style. A glass atrium covers the lobby which is surrounded by a series of arched balconies and interior courtyards. At the rear, a series of terraces and hanging gardens tumble down scenically; in the eaves there's a tiny pool and sauna; in the basement cavernous cellars. Public spaces and salons are decorated with audacious confidence. It's a stunner.

C'est si bon!

A quartet of Renaissance
buildings with the
Wow factor.

Bon repos Rooms are seductive and theatrical; and how. Opulent schemes combine velvets, silks, damasks and linens; antiques, tapestries and objets d'art juxtapose modern furniture and art. Bathrooms, designed by Starck, boast double baths, jacuzzis, and power showers.

Bon appetit Lyon is France's gastronomic capital, and cooking at the hotel's Café Epicerie not surprisingly dazzles. Classical techniques are used in eclectic menus: grilled Brittany lobster tail with Japanese red shiso cress; saddle of rabbit with beetroot; scallops with poached rhubarb. Expect terrific breakfasts, too.

Bon temps Lyon buzzes. It's a UNESCO World Heritage site so culture vultures have rich pickings. There's Vieux Lyons, the Basilica, 18th century silk weaver's houses, museums galore, lovely river walks and markets. Explore Beaujolais and Rhône vineyards; sample France's greatest concentration of Michelin restaurants. You want more?

Bon voyage 15 minutes by taxi from TGV station.

Château de Bagnols

69620 Bagnols-en-Beaujolais
Tel: +33 (0) 4 74 71 40 00
Fax: +33 (0) 4 74 71 40 49
info@bagnols.com
www.roccofortehotels.com

Rooms and rates
12 rooms, 8 suites
Double room for 2 people
per night from €425 to €1,300
Breakfast €17. Dinner from €70

General manager
Franco Mora

Open
All year except 2 Jan – 31 Mar

Château de Bagnols is gorgeous enough to make you believe in fairytales. Framed by Beaujolais vineyards and hills, it dates in part back to the 13th century. Restorations by owner Lady Hamlyn have unearthed old Renaissance decorations amidst the old honey-coloured stone (one Gothic fireplace is the biggest of its kind in Europe). Rooms boast antique furniture of museum quality. Everything glows. A moat and drawbridge, terraces, parkland and every luxurious comfort complete this idyll. Service is immaculate, and for all its opulence the château contrives to feel relaxed and private. We adored it.

C'est si bon!

Burgundian heaven worth splashing out for.

Bon repos Rooms are the stuff of romance (honeymooners, take note). Suites are divinely decorated, and some boast original Renaissance wall paintings. Four-posters are draped with shimmering period silks and velvets, while the rooms in the old stable have views to die for.

Bon appetit The château's Michelin-starred Salle des Gardes sees chef Matthieu Fontaine exemplify gastronomy the area's famous for. Expect traditional specialities working with the seasons, spit-roasted game and seductive contemporary dishes. The wine list is profound.

Bon temps Explore nearby Lyon with its Vieille Ville, museums and great restaurants. Follow vine trails through Beaujolais and Burgundy countryside and stop in pretty Romanesque villages; lose yourself in the château's landscaped park with its circular pool; or try tennis, golf, riding and balloon rides nearby.

Bon voyage From Lyon: take the A6 to Limonest, then join D485. Pass through Lozanne, then turn right onto the D38.

Château d'Igé

Route du Château
71960 Igé
Tel: +33 (0) 3 85 33 33 99
Fax: +33 (0) 3 85 33 41 41
ige@chateauxhotels.com
www.chateaudige.com

Rooms and rates
8 rooms, 6 apartments
Double room for 2 people
per night from €93 to €144
Breakfast €14. Dinner from €35

Proprietor
Françoise Germond-Lieury

Open
1 March - 30 November

This ancient creeper-clad and turreted manor in southern Burgundy was built by the counts of Mâcon. It's surrounded by parkland and exuberant flowerbeds, and flanked by a stream filled with trout and willows dipping into the water. The bridge crossing has now become a gorgeous terrace with tables, while a charming winter garden also beckons the outside in. Once you're in, there are thick stone walls and floors, wooden beams, vast fireplaces and winding staircases – all providing a backdrop to elegant furnishings. Owner Françoise Germond-Lieury and her staff exude friendliness. So what are you waiting for?

C'est si bon!

Burgundian beauty steeped in feudal castle charm.

Bon repos Bed down in a room at the top of a tower with vaulted ceiling and leaded windows, toile de Jouy clad walls, vases of flowers and Empire furniture. Opt for a four-poster bed, perhaps, or the suite created from a former chapel. Add the champagne on ice and it's time to lock the door...

Bon appetit Guests are spoilt for choice: chef Olivier Pons' prize-winning Burgundian gastronomy can be enjoyed in the Fireplace room, Blue room, Red room, conservatory or terrace. Menus include a Surprise Dégustation (course course after course of delectables), to be washed down with an excellent Burgundy, sans doute.

Bon temps What peachy countryside! Woods, wild meadows, gentle hills and vineyards beckon. Follow hiking trails, or try cultural ones taking in Cluny's ancient abbey, Cormatin's famous château and Romanesque churches. Take Mâconnais and Beaujolais wine tours or swim, ride and golf.

Bon voyage From Lyon: take N6 to Macon and N79 towards Cluny. Follow signs to La Roche Vineuse, Verzé and Igé.

Auberge du Bois Prin

Les Moussoux
74400 Chamonix
Tel: +33 (0) 4 50 53 33 51
Fax: +33 (0) 4 50 53 48 75
info@boisprin.com
www.boisprin.com

Rooms and rates
11 rooms
Double room for 2 people
per night from €138 to €219
Breakfast included. Dinner from €28

Proprietors
Denis and Monique Carrier

Open
27 Nov – 12 April, 7 May – 24 Oct

It's all downhill at this famous Savoy ski resort, but the Bois Prin neatly keeps its end up minutes from Chamonix. During the season this handsome three-storey pine chalet is surrounded by blue-tinted snowdrifts but come summer the valley's green again, scented with gentian. The location's terrific too, with an unhindered aspect towards France's highest mountain. Owners Denis and Monique Carrier run a friendly place, and the terrace is definitely a winner, trapping sun amidst fresh Alpine air. This is a place to slip out of those salopettes, have a hot-tub soak or a sauna and enjoy the bar's après-ski camaraderie.

C'est si bon!

Wake up to Mont Blanc – every room boasts a view.

Bon repos Follow your mountain adventures by sinking into long hot baths and the comfiest of beds. Pine surrounds and typical Savoyard decor increase the Alpine ambience. All rooms (some with carved wooden balconies) offer marvellous views of Mont Blanc.

Bon appetit Taste-packed home-grown herbs and produce are a feature of Denis's cooking, with inventive takes on local cuisine. Drink fine Mondeuse or Apremont wines (not far to stagger upstairs should you get piste), nibble creamy Reblochon cheeses and freshly-baked breads. Breakfasting on the panoramic terrace gives added meal appeal.

Bon temps Skiing's the thing, but not exclusively. Descend into the Vallée Blanche, master the snowboarding pistes on the Brevant and Grand Montets, go mountain biking, swim and try Alpine rafting. Or simply play golf, check out Chamonix, and walk or picnic on pretty mountain trails.

Bon voyage From Geneva: take the A40 to exit marked Chamonix South. Follow signs to hotel or Les Moussoux.

Hôtel Mont Blanc

Place de l'Eglise
74120 Megève
Tel: +33 (0) 4 50 21 20 02
Fax: +33 (0) 4 50 21 45 28
contact@hotelmontblanc.com
www.c-h-m.com

Rooms and rates
29 rooms, 11 suites
Double room for 2 people
per night from €160 to €354
Breakfast €15

General manager
Jocelyne Sibuet

Open
All year round except May

There are French Alp resorts and then there's Megève: old money, quiet glamour and the Mont Blanc. This classy Alpine chalet in the unspoilt town centre is now as much a landmark as the snow-covered mountain it's named after. Owners Jean-Louis and Jocelyne Sibuet took hold of a century-old ruin and made it drop-dead chic. Blond pine and oak panelling throughout glow invitingly. The confident mix of English country house, aristocratic Austrian and trad Haute Savoie styles works a treat. A charming interior courtyard and tiny pool (only open in summer) complete this alpine idyll. Talk about a romantic high!

C'est si bon!

Glossy French Alps chalet where style reaches its peak.

Bon repos Cosy meets plush in gorgeously appointed rooms, displaying a fabulous eye for detail. Honey-coloured panelling forms a warm backdrop to well-dressed beds, rich soft furnishings and furniture, fashionable fabrics and perky Savoyard plaids. Very 'pulled together' and deeply, deeply comfortable.

Bon appetit A charming Tyrolean-styled breakfast room kickstarts the day (with style, naturellement). Traditional afternoon tea in the drawing room has become a social fixture, as are drinks on the terrace in fine weather. No question that après-ski and dining here are the smartest.

Bon temps Whatever the season, tired lungs come alive with mountain air. In winter, head for the piste; all skis, snowshoes, slalom and horse-drawn sleighs. In spring and summer slopes are flower-filled, so traipse them or picnic. Play golf, tennis and ride – or spend packets at posh antique and designer shops.

Bon voyage From Geneva: take A40-E25; exit Sallanches.

l'Auberge du Choucas

Rue de la Fruitière
05220 Monetier les Bains
Tel: +33 (0) 4 92 24 42 73
Fax: +33 (0) 4 92 24 51 60
auberge.du.choucas@wanadoo.fr
www.aubergeduchoucas.com

Rooms and rates
8 rooms, 4 apartments
Double room for 2 people
per night from €100 to €185
Breakfast €15. Dinner from €39

Proprietor
Nicole Sánchez-Ventura

Open
11 Dec – 1 May and 29 May – 30 Oct

Photography: ELIOPHOT

Snug in the foothills of the snow-capped Ecrins National Park, L'Auberge du Choucas offers peace and the sunniest of welcomes in chocolate-box surroundings. The charm of this 17th century converted farmhouse, tucked beside a 500-year-old church, lies in its quaint bonhomie. It's the sort of place where clean mountain air blends with the enticing aroma of home cooking to permeate the stone-walled lounge and up the wooden staircase. Guests repairing from a hard day's slog on the piste or simply wanting somewhere to curl up by the fireside with a book, might be hard pushed to find anything as enticingly homely as this.

C'est si bon!

Clinking crystal glasses and crackling log fires break the ice beautifully.

Bon repos Deceptively spacious but cosy bedrooms, many with balconies perfect for breathing in all that fresh mountain air, make the midnight stretch up the stairs just that bit more pleasurable. Rugs, oak furniture and wood panelling add alpine warmth.

Bon appetit Daily changing menus from the surprisingly creative young chef might include – depending on season – pavé de truite de mer or tournedos de canard avec poires caramelisées. Guests dine in pretty candlelit surrounds.

Bon temps Numerous winter sports are for the taking here in the ski domain of Serre-Chevalier. When you're done on the slopes, melt away in one of the warm thermal spa pools just minutes away. Or – depending on the season – get booted up and head for walking trails, pine forests and scenic cable car rides – or stretch out on your terrace and bliss out in that Alpine sunshine.

Bon voyage From Geneva: take the A41/N91 to Grenoble and Briançon. Hotel is behind church, in front of the Mairie.

Provence & Côte d'Azur:
from the Camargue to Monte Carlo

Aller for glamorous getaways
Manger bouillabaisse, garlicky aïoli dips
Santé! pastis with ice

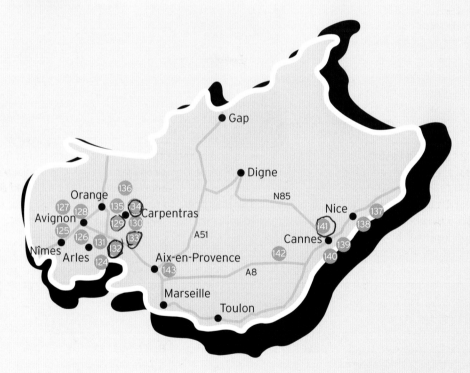

Gap

Digne

Orange
136
N85
127 128 135 134
Nice
137
Avignon Carpentras
138
125 129 130
141
126 131 133
Cannes
139
Nîmes 132
142
140
Arles A51
124
Aix-en-Provence
143
A8
Marseille
Toulon

Roads ———

Pages 124 – 143

Why?

Hedonistic beach culture fringes the mélange of Med and country that makes up Provence and the Côte d'Azur. Behind the fabled Riviera playground of the rich and famous, where the bronzed and the beautiful come to play in their sleek yachts and Belle Epoch villas, lies old Provence: countryside studded with medieval hilltop villages, Roman antiquities and purple fields of lavender.

So why not...♥

- Schmooze with the starry-eyed on the Cannes Croisette
- Bronze with the jeunesse dorée on private beaches
- Dine out in the backstreet cafés and bistros of Old Nice
- Play pelote with the locals in village squares
- See the salt marshes, white horses, cowboys and flamingos of the Camargue

Le Mas de Peint

Le Sambuc
13200 Arles
Tel: +33 (0) 4 90 97 20 62
Fax: +33 (0) 4 90 97 22 20
contact@masdepeint.com
www.masdepeint.com

Rooms and rates
8 rooms, 3 suites
Double room/suite for 2 people
per night from €197 to €378
Breakfast €19. Dinner from €43

Proprietors
Jacques and Lucille Bon

Open
Except 10 Jan-18 Mar, 19 Nov-19 Dec

The glorious Camargue – that wild expanse of salt marshes between Arles and Marseille – is the Mediterranean's Wild West, complete with cowboys on horseback, black bulls and a blur of pink flamingoes. Not that staying out in this neck of the woods need mean roughing it. Check into the luxurious Camargue ranch Le Mas de Peint, and wild horses won't drag you away. This former 17th century barn is a supremely hip address which regularly graces the pages of lifestyle magazines. Madame Bon's passion for antiques – dressers, washstands, old bullfighting prints and riding memorabilia – lends rustic sophistication and lashings of character.

C'est si bon!

Sumptuous setting for untamed Wild West thrills.

Bon repos Many of the sumptuously spacious bedrooms have brass beds, gnarled beams, and double-ended cast-iron baths with linen-fronted shower cloaks. Some bathrooms are built on galleries overlooking the sleeping quarters, while the private Terrasse suite is a favourite with lovers.

Bon appetit Watch the chef knocking up delicious southern dishes with a modern twist in the open farmhouse-style kitchen-dining room. Garden-fresh herbs, home-reared beef and chicken and daily landed fish are mainstays of the menu. Regulars include risotto with green asparagus and parmesan shavings, and red mullet with fresh basil.

Bon temps Here's your chance to saddle up and tour a working ranch on horseback or in the back of a 4x4 – an unmissable experience. You're on the doorstep of a national park, so look out for kingfishers, herons and a wealth of wild flowers. Historic Arles is a 30-minute drive.

Bon voyage From Marseille: take the A8/A54 to Arles, then D36 to Salin de Giraud. The ranch is 500m after Sambuc.

l'Hacienda

Le Mas de Brignon
30320 Marguerittes
Tel: +33 (0) 4 66 75 02 25
Fax: +33 (0) 4 66 75 45 58
contact@hotel-hacienda-nimes.com
www.hotel-hacienda-nimes.com

Rooms and rates
12 rooms
Double room for 2 people
per night from €70 to €140
Breakfast €12-15. Dinner from €30

Proprietor
Jean-Jacques Chauvin

Open
Mid March - late October

L'Hacienda is reached by a small country road lined with vineyards and olive groves. This is the Languedoc at its most peaceful, where the region meets Provence and the Camargue. As the name suggests it looks a little Spanish: a long, low villa with white walls and shutters, tiled roof and terracotta floors that also incorporates an attractive old turret. Surrounded by red hibiscus, it surveys fields of lavender. The scent drifts over guests who invariably find themselves draped on terrace loungers or around the pool. The mood is languid; it's easy to fall into a state of mañana here. Thankfully, charming owners the Chauvins, don't.

C'est si bon!

Ready to chill? This tranquil hacienda near Nîmes has your name on it.

Bon repos Beamed rooms with white walls and tiled red floors are simply and cheerfully decorated, but don't neglect comfort. Many open on to their own sunny terrace – ideal for siestas after an indulgent long lunch.

Bon appetit Zingingly fresh ingredients bought daily from local provençal markets provide dishes with dense flavours and resonance. Depending on the season, meals are served either in the rustic candlelit dining room or on the terrace by the pool.

Bon temps You're well situated for sightseeing here: check out Le Pont du Gard's Roman aqueduct; the Nîmes-Arles-Avignon historic triangle; fortified Aigues-Mortes; the Cévennes hills; the hiking trails of the Gardon; or boating, fishing and bathing in the Ardèche. Play boules or table-tennis on site, or try riding, tennis and golf nearby.

Bon voyage From Exit 24 (Nîmes Est) of the A9 take the D86. Once in the village of Marguerittes (three miles) , follow the red signs.

adran Solaire

Cabaret Neuf
Graveson
+33 (0) 4 90 95 71 79
Fax: +33 (0) 4 90 90 55 04
cadransolaire@wanadoo.fr
www.hotel-en-provence.com

Rooms and rates
12 rooms
Double room for 2 people
per night from €54 to €76
Breakfast €7.

Proprietors
Sophie and Olivier Guilmet

Open
Most of the year; check in winter

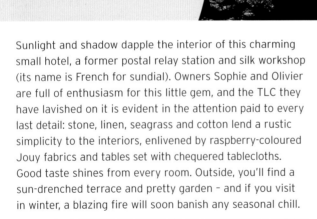

Sunlight and shadow dapple the interior of this charming small hotel, a former postal relay station and silk workshop (its name is French for sundial). Owners Sophie and Olivier are full of enthusiasm for this little gem, and the TLC they have lavished on it is evident in the attention paid to every last detail: stone, linen, seagrass and cotton lend a rustic simplicity to the interiors, enlivened by raspberry-coloured Jouy fabrics and tables set with chequered tablecloths. Good taste shines from every room. Outside, you'll find a sun-drenched terrace and pretty garden – and if you visit in winter, a blazing fire will soon banish any seasonal chill.

C'est si bon!

Chic and cheerful;
brilliant for lovebirds
on a budget.

Bon repos Sweet dreams are promised in the hotel's 12 comfortable double bedrooms. Each has its own zest and style (artist Sophie has designed them individually) and all are fresh and restful, decorated in pleasing provençal fabrics and colours.

Bon appetit Enjoy breakfast outside on the terrace or in the large, bright breakfast room. Venture out to Graveson's famous farmers' market to stock up on wine, goat's cheese and fresh fruit for a picnic lunch. Your hosts will be pleased to recommend an intimate little bistro for dinner.

Bon temps There's plenty to do in Graveson and the surrounds, with churches, castles and museums to explore. You're just a short drive from the delightful provençal towns of St Rémy and Les Baux. You could also head for historic Arles, visit a perfume factory or push deeper into the long-grass countryside of the Camargue.

Bon voyage From Avignon, follow the D28 towards Arles and Tarascon. Signposted on the approach to Graveson.

La Mirande

4 place de la Mirande
84000 Avignon
Tel: +33 (0) 4 90 85 93 93
Fax: +33 (0) 4 90 86 26 85
mirande@la-mirande.fr
www.la-mirande.fr

Rooms and rates
18 rooms, 2 suites
Double room for 2 people
per night from €280 to €450
Breakfast from €20. Dinner from €49

General manager
Martin Stein

Open
All year round

Photos: Nicolas Bruant

Chic, boutique and achingly cool – that's La Mirande, buried deep inside the walls of ancient Avignon. Originally the private residence of a leading famille bourgeoise, it's now a rivetingly stylish hotel whose original 18th century features have been gilded with contemporary flair. No detail has been missed in the refurbishment of this Louis XVI townhouse, whose rooms are clustered around a moodily lit inner courtyard and regularly grace the pages of glossy magazines. Style slaves will enjoy celebrity spotting in the bar and clocking the meticulously crafted design details.

C'est si bon!

Ravishing address for the cash-to-splash hotel cognoscenti.

Bon repos Prepare to be smitten; we were. Wall coverings are specially commissioned copies of 18th century originals; lamps glow amid antique furnishings, and lavish marble-tiled bathrooms pander to indulgence. The best look out on to the floodlit Pope's palace or secluded rear town garden.

Bon appetit Guests dine on classic French cuisine beneath wooden beams in a chandeliered dining room hung with old masters. The sheltered garden makes a divine setting for intimate suppers on a summer's night. Should you hanker after company, you can always join the manager's convivial dinner table in the old kitchens downstairs.

Bon temps A walk down cobbled back streets takes you straight to the Pope's palace, Avignon's finest historic monument. Other landmarks abound and if you tire of sightseeing and smart stores, head off to the lovely provençal towns of Pont-du-Gard, Arles and Les Baux.

Bon voyage 10 minutes by taxi from TGV station. If driving (tricky), call hotel for detailed directions.

Hôtel de l'Atelier

5 rue de la Foire
30400 Villeneuve-les-Avignon
Tel: +33 (0) 4 90 25 01 84
Fax: +33 (0) 4 90 25 80 06
hotel-latelier@libertysurf.fr
www.hoteldelatelier.com

Rooms and rates
23 rooms
Double room for 2 people
per night from €46 to €91
Breakfast €8

Proprietors
Annick and Gérard Burret

Open
All year round

This original 16th century artist's workshop sits in the centre of Villeneuve-les-Avignon, a hillside town whose pleasing facades and squares lie a few miles from Avignon proper. As you might expect the house is suffused with light, and even today, it's the setting for many travelling exhibitions of pictures and sculptures. The interior shows a restrained palette of colour; there's lots of old polished wood and on cool evenings, a blazing fire warms the stylish salon. On warm days guests can cool off on the terrace and shaded garden (which, incidentally, is pretty enough to sketch). This is a long, long way from the garret of old.

C'est si bon!

Once a run-down artist's studio, it paints a pretty picture today.

Bon repos Individual rooms have a chic simplicity, many with beams and stone floors. Colours are restful and muted: shades of white predominate, with plum or terracotta accents. Large windows let in streams of light. All have good bathrooms, some with twin basins.

Bon appetit Breakfast is served in the cheerful dining room, and on the patio in warm weather. Your hosts are happy to point you towards some of the local dining hotspots for dinner.

Bon temps Avignon is on the doorstep, with its rich papal history, chi-chi stores and sights. There's a stunning view of the city (and its famous bridge) from the top of the 14th century Philippe le Bel Tower. Markets abound – try the Provençal on Thursday and Brocantes on Saturdays – or browse the 400-odd shops and stalls at L'Isle Sur La Sorgue, southern France's biggest antiques centre.

Bon voyage From Avignon: cross the river via Pont Daladier and turn first right. Follow signs to Villeneuve town centre.

Domaine du Prieuré de Margoye

1283 chemin de Margoye
84800 L'Isle sur la Sorgue
Tel: +33 (0) 4 90 20 81 51
Fax: +33 (0) 4 90 20 84 08
carole@prieure-provence.com
www.prieure-provence.com

Rooms and rates
4 rooms
Double room for 2 people
per night from €100 to €180
Breakfast included. Dinner from €30

Proprietors
Carole and Joël Gayet

Open
All year round

What makes this dreamy stopover work? First, the priory itself – simple and stylish within, and set off by surrounds dating back to the 17th century. Then there's the setting: grounds sprawling across the Margoye plateau of the Vaucluse, with uninterrupted views of rolling provençal hills. Summer-time stays revolve around a stunning stone 'infinity pool', flanked by perfumed pine and almond trees, with scented herbs underfoot, the hum of cicadas in the grass and the clink of champagne glasses while you sway gently in hammocks (blame the breeze, not the bubbly!). Owners Carole and Joël Gayet are the most sociable hosts.

C'est si bon!

Ancient priory in a devilishly pretty setting.

Bon repos Rooms are done out in impeccable and sparing style. No frills or flounces here: expect king-size beds, good linens, scented candles, quality toiletries and even a fridge (for that bubbly). The huge Quinson suite, with its Victorian cast-iron bathtub, 180 degree views and polished wood floor, is big enough to lose yourself in.

Bon appetit Sumptuous breakfasts provide home-made bread and jams, Viennoiseries, cheeses and fruits. Twice a week in July and August there's a candlelit buffet in the pretty courtyard. In the wintry truffle season owner Carole shaves the local black gold into omelettes.

Bon temps Explore idyllic countryside, museums, antique shops, flea markets and brocante fairs. Work up a sweat with mountain climbing (go on!) cycling and riding. Stay put in the Prieuré for some lazy pétanque, golf practice, or to go to some lengths in the 20m pool.

Bon voyage From Avignon: take N7/D22 towards Apt and N100 to L'Isle sur la Sorgue. Turn right to Margoye.

Domaine des Granges du Bosquet

1473 Chemin du Bosquet
84800 l'Isle sur la Sorgue
Tel: +33 (0) 4 90 21 19 89
Fax: +33 (0) 4 90 21 52 06
contact@gdb-provence.com
www.gdb-provence.com

Rooms and rates
7 apartments
Double room for 2 people
per night from €100 to €205
Breakfast included

Proprietors
Réjane and Richard Mortreux

Open
All year round

Your hosts, Réjane and Richard, originally hail from the north of France, but fell in love with this ancient stone-built cluster of farm buildings. They have transformed it with style and verve into a collection of indulgently spacious apartments, infused with the delights of provençal art de vivre. Sculptures are scattered through the grounds, where the sounds of cicadas and the mistral rustling through the olive trees mixes with the heady scent of lavender. Réjane is great company and makes you feel like a cherished guest in the home of old friends. This place will leave you blissed out, loved up and (just possibly) chained down.

C'est si bon!

Adventures start in the Marquis de Sade room, complete with cuffs and chains...

Bon repos Take your pick from rooms and apartments oozing chic and named after writers of romantic renown. Elegant, classical Petrarque combines puritanism with passion, while La Picholine is a traditional and private provençal cottage. For those feeling more risqué, there's Sade - named after the notoriously red-blooded Marquis himself- complete with opulent chandelier, wild leopardskin print bathroom, four-poster and (mais oui!) chains.

Bon appetit Book a superb meal, prepared in the grande cuisine tradition, or browse the local markets for olives, patés, bread, wine and fruit for a gourmet picnic à deux.

Bon temps Top up your tan by the pool, or loll beneath an almond tree for an afternoon siesta. Take a cycle ride along countryside paths, book a game of golf, saddle up and head for the hills, or paddle your own canoe on the Sorgue river - and indulge in a relaxing massage afterwards.

Bon voyage From Lyon: Leave A7 at Avignon Sud, follow D22 through L'Isle sur la Sorgue towards Apt; signed right.

La Riboto de Taven

Le Val d'Enfer
13520 Les Baux de Provence
Tel: +33 (0) 4 90 54 34 23
Fax: +33 (0) 4 90 54 38 88
contact@riboto-de-taven.fr
www.riboto-de-taven.fr

Rooms and rates
6 rooms
Double room for 2 people
per night from €152 to €200
Breakfast €16. Dinner €46

Proprietors
The Novi-Thème family

Open
March - January

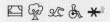

Maybe the locals were having a tongue-in-cheek joke when this cliffy enclave was christened the Valley of Hell. We'd say it's closer to the Garden of Eden. Christine, Philippe and Jean Pierre Novi-Thème's little paradise lies in the dip below Les Baux de Provence, a medieval cliff-top village with views the devil would sell his soul for. It's not just the handsome old building itself that makes it a stunner, but the richly dramatic rooms in the troglodyte caves above. There's also a gorgeous pool, leafy grounds that suddenly erupt into towering cliffs, friendly hosts and a congenial restaurant. Swish, stylish and secluded: we loved it.

C'est si bon!

The address is the Valley of Hell – but this is a little provençal paradise.

Bon repos Here's your chance to bed down in one of two troglodyte cave rooms, carved out of the rock face and theatrically furnished with canopied beds and softest comforts. Rooms and suites within the farmhouse are more conventional but no less desirable. Enjoy spectacular views all round.

Bon appetit Dinner here is worth waiting for: The Novi-Thème's have evolved their own home-style provençal cuisine with devotion and rigour. Zingy market produce is cooked in the estate's own home-produced olive oil, and flavoured with morning-fresh herbs and aromatic infusions. Pick a lusty Côtes de Baux as accompaniment.

Bon temps There's plenty to occupy you here, with dips in the pool, walks in the valley, browsing in markets or in the galleries of Les Baux, and exploring any number of old towns and villages for cultural diversions.

Bon voyage From St Rémy de Provence: D5 to Maussane and D27 to Les Baux. Turn right downhill just after village.

Mas doù Pastré

Quartier Saint Sixte
13810 Eygalières
Tel: +33 (0) 4 90 95 92 61
Fax: +33 (0) 4 90 90 61 75
contact@masdoupastre.com
www.masdoupastre.com

Rooms and rates
11 rooms, 1 suite
Double room for 2 people
per night from €95 to €190
Breakfast €12. Dinner €32

Proprietors
Albine and Maurice Roumanille

Open
Except 15 November - 15 December

What a cracker. This trio of characterful provençal buildings still displays 18th century origins. Once a cattle byre, it's been handed down through generations of the same family and is now artfully run - and brilliantly designed - by Maurice and Albine Roumanille. The place glows in uplifting traditional colours. Each room is differently and imaginatively styled (we loved them all), with rustic furniture, gorgeous fabrics and antiques trawled from nearby markets. Guests can idle away summer days slunk in a deck chair or cooling off in the pool. You can even bed down in your own private Romany caravan at the bottom of the garden.

C'est si bon!

Blissful Provençal outpost packed with rustic chic.

Bon repos Rooms have flair and originality, not to mention dishy bathrooms with shiny chrome fittings. Each has its own charm and personality, and most have terraces. If you're keen to bring out the gypsy in your soul, spend a fun night in one of the vintage wooden caravans.

Bon appetit Breakfast here is a treat, with freshly-baked goodies, thick home-made jams, Albine's own fromage blanc and quince jelly. Simple suppers are mouthwatering and bursting with provençal flavours. Guests often linger over a digestif in the garden's lavender-laden night air, where only the hum of cicadas disturbs the peace.

Bon temps First visit the nearby Chapelle Saint-Sixte, then pray for perfect conditions to ramble in the scenic Alpilles. Poke around in the markets and antique fairs of nearby L'Isle sur la Sorgue, explore cultural spots such as Aix, Arles, and Avignon, swim or play boules in the garden.

Bon voyage From the A7, travel via Cavaillon and St Rémy. The Mas is half a mile beyond Eygalières village.

Bastide de Voulonne

84220 Cabrières d'Avignon
Tel: +33 (0) 4 90 76 77 55
Fax: +33 (0) 4 90 76 77 56
sophie@bastide-voulonne.com
www.bastide-voulonne.com

Rooms and rates
8 rooms, 1 suite
Double room for 2 people
per night from €122 to €145
Breakfast €11. Dinner €29

Proprietors
Sophie and Alain Rebourg

Open
Except 14 Nov - 20 Dec

This charming 18th century farmhouse is decorated in earth tones and natural fabrics as warm as the welcome you'll receive from hosts Sophie and Alain, who fell in love with the house and have breathed new life and colour into it. Boldly patterned provençal fabrics, wrought iron and an eclectic mix of furniture combine to create a look that's intimate but up-to-the-minute; cosy but chic. Bow windows allow the sun to pour into these graciously proportioned rooms, tempting you out onto the terrace to doze by the splashing fountain. From there, fields of lavender stretch towards the Luberon mountains. This is the life!

C'est si bon!

Homespun charm, warm hospitality and food just like maman makes.

Bon repos Terracotta-tiled floors, king-size beds, beamed ceilings and softly draped curtains exude a rustic charm that invites you to snuggle down and get better acquainted.

Bon appetit Enjoy an aperitif by the fountain before wandering into the dining room, where a blazing fire will banish any evening chill. Hearty provençal cuisine in the 'bonne femme' style is served up by Alain, who trawls the markets each morning in search of fresh local produce. Linger over breakfast in the courtyard during summer.

Bon temps Any sense of ennui is kept firmly at bay here, with a range of activities laid on for those keen to do more than read a book or stroll hand-in-hand through the village. You'll find yourself becoming an expert on olives, sampling the local wines and even embarking on a hunt for those precious, musk-scented black truffles.

Bon voyage From the A7, take the D2 for Cavaillon. Join the RN100 for Apt, and turn off at Coustellet for Gordes.

Château de Mazan

Place Napoléon
84380 Mazan
Tel: +33 (0) 4 90 69 62 61
Fax: +33 (0) 4 90 69 76 62
contact@chateaudemazan.fr
www.chateaudemazan.fr

Rooms and rates
30 rooms
Double room for 2 people
per night from €90 to €255
Breakfast €15. Dinner from €48

Proprietor
Frédéric Lhermie

Open
8 March - 31 December

Few places can claim more pleasures of the flesh than Château de Mazan, once home to the father of the infamous Marquis de Sade. What louche tales these walls might tell! Today those self-same walls - well-behaved in pink, peach and apricot - bounce sensuous provençal light off shiny marble floors while good furniture gleams in airy salons. The Marquis would likely have strolled the gorgeous grounds, though it's hard to fathom how his unchained imagination was fired by the profusion of lavender and santolina, or the shady mulberry trees. We reckon he'd agree that Mazan metes out exquisite punishment.

C'est si bon!

Provençal château with
the decidedly upper hand.

Bon repos Your spacious and elegant room in quiet pastels might contain a four-poster, open onto a flowered terrace or even its own private garden. Some enjoy views over village rooftops. Baths have steam showers or jacuzzis. Be naughty (the Marquis would approve).

Bon appetit The château's L'Ingénue restaurant - originally the setting for de Sade's plays - is pretty, soft-coloured and candlelit. Today the drama comes from Iris Enrich's cooking, with exemplary dishes such as scallops with coconut milk and black truffles or roast partridge with bilberries. There's a lovely terrace for summer dining.

Bon temps Follow the Route de Vins vineyards, or take excursions to Avignon's Palais des Papes, Mont Ventoux and the Luberon's wild landscape and pretty villages. Antique hunt at L'Isle-sur-la-Sorgue. Wander the château's landscaped gardens, swim in the pool or play golf.

Bon voyage From Avignon: take the D942 for Carpentras, Mont Ventoux and Mazan. Turn right after the Mairie.

Château Talaud

84870 Loriol du Comtat
Tel: +33 (0) 4 90 65 71 00
Fax: +33 (0) 4 90 65 77 93
chateautalaud@infonie.fr
www.chateautalaud.com

Rooms and rates
4 rooms, 1 suite
Double room for 2 people
per night from €155 to €195
Breakfast included
Dinner from €40

Proprietors
Hein and Conny Deiters-Kommer

Open
March - December

No gargoyles here – angelic cupids adorn the walls of this 18th century château, which lies in the heart of Provence, surrounded by its own vineyards. Indoors, precious antiques rub shoulders with modern comforts; graceful curves of wrought iron, polished wooden floors, high ceilings and walls adorned with original works of art lend the rooms an air of comfort and expensive elegance. It's a place that oozes tradition, yet has all the hallmarks of contemporary flair. Owners Hein and Conny are the friendliest couple, and with only five rooms, you may just feel as if this little world has been created for your exclusive pleasure.

C'est si bon!

Sipping an aperitif next to the fountain as the sun sets is de rigueur.

Bon repos Bedrooms here are named after their colour, so you could find yourself surrounded by soothing blue, warm yellow, sage green or vibrant cherry. Expect noble proportions, light streaming through the windows and the scent of fresh flowers... a blissful boudoir, no less.

Bon appetit Tables and chaise-longues are dotted around the gardens, so you can enjoy an ample breakfast or an aperitif in the sunshine. Don't forget to try a glass of the ruby-red Côtes du Ventoux produced from the hotel's own vineyard. For dinner, your hosts Hein and Conny will recommend one of the many excellent local restaurants.

Bon temps Cool off in the pool in warm weather, or head for Avignon, Aix-en-Provence, Nîmes and Saint Rémy (where there's a weekly treasure-trove of a market). Wine-tasting possibilities abound, and there's no shortage of galleries and boutiques nearby for browsing.

Bon voyage From Avignon: take D942 for Carpentras, then D107 at Monteux-Est; turn off for Loriol du Comtat.

effroi

, Cité Médiévale
Romaine
0 36 04 71
Fax: +33 (0) 4 90 36 24 78
lebeffroi@wanadoo.fr
www.le-beffroi.com

Rooms and rates
22 rooms
Double room for 2 people
per night from €85 to €125
Breakfast €12. Dinner from €26

Proprietors
Christine and Yann Christiansen

Open
Late March – late January

Standing within sight of Mont Ventoux, this former Roman town is steeped in charm and antiquity. The same might easily be said of 16th century Le Beffroi, managed by Yann Christiansen and his partner Christine. An original limestone spiral staircase makes a dramatic statement, as does the tall beamed salon hung with chandeliers and decorated with antiques. It feels Italianate, almost like the private quarters of a doge's palace. There's a conservatory leading onto a delightful creeper-clad garden and a flower-decked terrace with recliners and a pool. Throw in the vistas and the floodlights at dusk, and it's all most fetching.

C'est si bon!

Superbly sited in one of Provence's medieval marvels.

Bon repos Rooms in the two adjoining wings provide stunning views of a skyline of old houses or terraced gardens where you can enjoy breakfast. Rooms are a good size and pleasantly done out, with modern comforts.

Bon appetit La Fontaine, the charming dining room, offers four good value prix-fixe and à la carte menus using seasonal produce. We relished scampi salad and fois gras ravioli followed by duck fillet in lavender honey and, to finish, crispy tarte Tatin. There's an excellent choice of local Côte du Rhône and Ventoux wines.

Bon temps Check out the town's scenic promenades and archaeological sites. Don't overlook hiking, riding, tennis and mini-golf, not to mention skiing in season. Then there's fifth century Seguret; the vineyards of Sablet; Gigondas' ancient citadel; Vacqueyras' château ramparts; and the caves of Beaumes de Venise.

Bon voyage From Nice: take the A7, then D942 (exit 23) and D938. At the town, follow signs to Cité Médiévale.

Le Royal Riviera

3 avenue Jean Monnet
06230 Saint-Jean-Cap-Ferrat
Tel: +33 (0) 4 93 76 31 00
Fax: +33 (0) 4 93 01 23 07
info@royal-riviera.com
www.royal-riviera.com

Rooms and rates
86 rooms, 7 suites
Double room for 2 people
per night from €185 to €675
Breakfast €25.50. Dinner from €48

General manager
Bruno Mercadal

Open
Mid January – late November

This swish hotel perches on the peninsular of exclusive Cap Ferrat. Imagine uninterrupted views of the Med, pristine beaches, landscaped gardens, orange groves and mountains. Bliss. But don't expect the predictable Belle Epoch look inside; recent renovations have given it contemporary appeal without ditching the building's inherent grandeur. Cool, muted colours lend an air of smart sophistication, while furniture and objets d'art are brought together in imaginative ways; be it ethnic, colonial, or in the case of the Grand Salon, neo-Hellenistic. The result is a slice of metropolitan chic in an unmistakably southern landscape.

C'est si bon!

Millionaire's playground on the Côte d'Azur makes guests feel mega-rich.

Bon repos Rooms, as you would expect, are ultra-spacious and come with every high-tech gadget. Choose between sea, garden or mountain views, or check out the ultra-private L'Orangerie, a villa with direct access to both pool and beach.

Bon appetit Share a plate of gourmet delicacies on the terrace of the Panorama restaurant with its knockout views of the Med; idly lounge poolside in the Pergola on hot summer days for perfectly chilled cocktails and something lightly grilled; or nibble late-night snacks in the striking Cap Bar with its oversized armchairs.

Bon temps It's a leisurely 15-minute stroll to the buzzing resort of Saint-Jean-Cap-Ferrat – that's if you're not playing tennis, golf or the roulette wheel (cover your stay with the winnings, perhaps?). Ditch the limousine and scale foothills to the gorgeous setting of Ephrussi de Rothschild.

Bon voyage Take the fast A8 or slower coastal road from Nice, six miles away. Follow signs when you reach the resort.

Hôtel Masséna

58 rue Gioffredo
06000 Nice
Tel: +33 (0) 4 92 47 88 88
Fax: +33 (0) 4 92 47 88 89
info@hotel-massena-nice.com
www.hotel-massena-nice.com

Rooms and rates
106 rooms
Double room for 2 people
per night from €90 to €190
Breakfast €15.

General manager
Anne Marie Quirin

Open
All year round

The British have loved Nice ever since they discovered the Côte d'Azur during Queen Victoria's reign. Some might find it a tad busy these days but most of us love it for that very buzz. While it may not be as flash as some big names on the Cannes Croisette, the Masséna has its own quiet glamour behind an impressive Belle Epoque facade, grandly lit at night. What's more, it's right at the heart of things; the Old Town, the Cours Saleya market and the parasols of that famous beach are just yards away. Tastefully decorated salons with hand-painted murals set the tone. Staff make a point of personable service. In short, extra nice.

C'est si bon!

When in Nice, here's one address that will do nicely.

Bon repos Rooms are comfortable and decorated in sunny provençal colours. Try and bag one with a balcony or terrace overlooking Nice, where you can slip into a complimentary bathrobe and sit there, come dusk, gazing at the lights of the coastline which twinkle all the way to Antibes. Then slip between crisp cotton sheets.

Bon appetit The cheerful breakfast room offers a generous morning buffet, but feel free to enjoy brekkie on your bedroom balcony. Round-the-clock room service is on hand should you require it. Nice doesn't lack for delicious seafood, and staff are happy to recommend the best places to dine al fresco à deux.

Bon temps Join the strollers and rollerbladers along the famed Promenade des Anglais and be sure to explore the lively Old Town just minutes away; shop till you drop; spend nights at the opera; visit museums; motor to Monte Carlo; play golf or get bronzed on the beach.

Bon voyage 15 minutes by taxi from Nice Airport; €28.

Hôtel Splendid

4 rue Félix Faure
06400 Cannes
Tel: +33 (0) 4 97 06 22 22
Fax: +33 (0) 4 93 99 55 02
accueil@splendid-hotel-cannes.fr
www.splendid-hotel-cannes.fr

Rooms and rates
62 rooms
Double room for 2 people
per night from €122 to €352
Breakfast €16

Director
Chantal Cagnat

Open
All year round

Flags flutter above this majestic icing-white building with terraces and gardens occupying a prime position in the centre of Cannes. To-die-for views over the yacht harbour, the Bay of Cannes and the Lerins islands reinforce the Hôtel Splendid's splendour. Its outward appearance might suggest formality but, as a family managed establishment, there's an emphasis on friendliness and good old-fashioned service amid the elegant home comforts of this century-old property. Don't miss the owner's collection of antique irons: a metaphor, perhaps, for the crease-free service guests receive.

C'est si bon!

Splendid by name, with splendiferous views.

Bon repos Staying up in the attic here pays dividends; there are two super suites whose views can't be topped. Rooms throughout are comfortably appointed, and those with harbour frontage have French windows and balconies. Plenty of 21st century technology keeps guests in touch.

Bon appetit Sitting on one of the bedroom's sea-facing balconies is a treat in itself. Start the day here or on the canopied terrace with a beautifully presented petit déjeuner, or sip a sundowner al fresco to plan nights out as day draws in.

Bon temps The glitzy film festival aside, there's something eternally glam about Cannes. Live it up with promenades (and star-spotting?) along the celebrated Croisette, shmooze on the perfectly kept plage or soak up the rays on yacht trips along the Côte d'Azur. Don't miss a stroll around the Vieille Ville, or a drive into the villages and scented hills behind the coast.

Bon voyage Follow signs to Vieux Port. TGV station 500m.

Le Cavendish

11 boulevard Carnot
06400 Cannes
Tel: +33 (0) 4 97 06 26 00
Fax: +33 (0) 4 97 06 26 01
reservation@cavendish-cannes.com
www.cavendish-cannes.com

Rooms and rates
34 rooms
Double room for 2 people
per night from €150 to €295
Breakfast €18

Proprietor
Christine Welter

Open
All year round

Lord Cavendish was declared 'the richest of intelligent men and the most intelligent of rich men' back in the mid 19th century. Such a forward-thinking gentleman would surely approve of the grand design created in this chic Cannes boutique hotel to which he has lent his name just a few minutes from La Croisette. Blending contemporary Riviera style with splashes of its aristocratic past - note the museum-piece lift, antique-filled salon and Carrara marble staircase - this newly refurbished haven of civility comes alive with the fiery rainbow reds and violets, blues and yellows so redolent of Provence.

C'est si bon!

Riviera chic with a dash of home-sweet-home charm.

Bon repos Lavender-scented pillows and a nibble of chocolate tease the senses as you retire to bed in coolly opulent rooms. The circular, soaring ceilings, king-size beds, marble showers and balconies of the Rotunda rooms hark back to the grandes demeures of the fin-de-siècle Riviera.

Bon appetit Breakfast is worth getting out of bed for, with home-made jams and pastries and plates of strawberries heaped high. Settle into a wicker chair later for English-style afternoon tea (choose from 15 blends) or a pre- or post-dinner drink from the bar - they're on the house to guests. Choose from dozens of chic eateries for dinner.

Bon temps Cannes is the party town of the jetset Côte d'Azur, with nightlife and shops to die for. Meander through the stalls of Forville market, take an island boat trip, or get bronzing with the bikinied throng on a private beach. Staff will reserve your sunbed and provide towels.

Bon voyage From Nice: leave A8, and follow signs to Centre Ville. Hotel is on right on boulevard Carnot. Valet parking.

Les Muscadins

18 boulevard Courteline
06250 Mougins
Tel: +33 (0) 4 92 28 28 28
Fax: +33 (0) 4 92 28 43 40
info@lemascandille.com
www.lemascandille.com

Rooms and rates
11 rooms
Double room for 2 people
per night from €139 to €399
Breakfast included. Dinner from €36

Director
Hubert Eurlings

Open
9 March - 31 October

What a pleasure to exit the autoroute and climb the 260 metres into Mougins, a gorgeous medieval village perched in olive, cypress and pine forests. Flowers grow here in profusion. What scents! And what sights, too. From here there's a panorama of the Bay of Cannes, Grasse and the Préalpes. How welcoming Les Muscadins looks: this small boutique property is pretty enough to paint (as Picasso did) and is home to a colony of gallery-owning artists and artisans. If this isn't enough, guests also have access to the luxurious Le Mas Candille, with its Shiseido Spa, a couple of minutes away. A double treat.

C'est si bon!

Magic at work in Mougins - guests quickly fall under Les Muscadins' spell.

Bon repos Rooms - some with balconies - are large, light and airy. Each has personalised decor and colours mirroring the sunny surroundings. Some look across to the Med, others over village streets. Breakfast is served both in the restaurant and on the terrace overlooking Cannes.

Bon appetit There is a bar for drinks, and classy cuisine on a flowery terrace. Dinner is served in the luminous restaurant where the chef harnesses the season's best ingredients in imaginative ways. There's more gastronomy at nearby Restaurant Candille or the poolside La Pergola. Decisions, decisions!

Bon temps Indulge yourselves around the two outdoor pools and jacuzzis, or become sybarites at the fabulous Shiseido Spa (Europe's first), all at the nearby Mas Candille. Head off deep into the Provence countryside or take the coastal road to the glam Côte d'Azur. Life's tough.

Bon voyage Take exit 42 from the A8 and Grasse-Mougins road at roundabout. Exit Mougins-Centre and follow signs.

Le Logis du Guetteur

Place du Château
83460 Les Arcs sur Argens
Tel: +33 (0) 4 94 99 51 10
Fax: +33 (0) 4 94 99 51 29
le.logis.du.guetteur@wanadoo.fr
www.logisduguetteur.com

Rooms and rates
10 rooms, 2 suites
Double room for 2 people
per night from €118 to €205
Breakfast €13. Dinner from €32

Proprietor
Max Callegari

Open
All year round

This is a place to soak up matchless views from a stone-flagged terrace surveying the Argens valley. Below you, an enticing pool terrace, a ramble of ancient rooftops and beyond, green hills stretching away. Around you, the stone walls dating back to the 11th century of an old watchman's house, complete with hilltop tower and cobbled courtyard. Enter by the old keep, and you're in an intriguing warren of old stairs and passages – one of which leads to the dramatically lit rough stone-walled restaurant. You'll be as relaxed as owner Max Callegari and his wife after a couple of days here.

C'est si bon!

Provençal hilltop roost with ace views in medieval setting.

Bon repos Air-conditioned rooms – many echoing views from the terrace – are individually decorated, with a mix of classic and modern touches. Cool tiled floors, uncluttered furniture and splashes of colour from modern oil paintings set the tone. Compact bathrooms are well kitted out.

Bon appetit Dining is the real treat here – whether it's out on the terrace, with its twinkling night views, or in the cave-like restaurant, whose candles, mood lighting, rough stone walls and crackling winter fires make it tailor-made for intimate dinners. Pick from starters such as spicy chilled gazpacho with fromage frais, and modish mains such as prawn tempura with fruit chutney and ginger. De-lish.

Bon temps You're just a short drive from the Verdon gorges to the north or lively Saint Tropez and the Med to the south. There's golf at Saint-Endreol and Thoronet Abbey close by, not to mention a score of pretty villages.

Bon voyage From Nice: take the A8 and join N7 at Le Muy, passing through Le Luc. On arrival, follow signs: vieille ville.

Villa Gallici

Avenue de la Violette
13100 Aix-en-Provence
Tel: +33 (0) 4 42 23 29 23
Fax: +33 (0) 4 42 96 30 45
gallici@relaischateaux.com
www.villagallici.com

Rooms and rates
18 rooms, 4 suites
Double room for 2 people
per night from €280 to €600
Breakfast €27. Dinner from €80

Director
Fabrice Mercier

Open
All year round

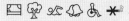

Cynics say true enchantment is elusive (or do they mean exclusive?). Either way Villa Gallici might change their minds. This 18th century Italianate mansion settled on the Bastide near the old quarter of Aix-en-Provence is heaving with charm. Tall cypress and plane trees frame terraces laden with statues, fountains, topiary and flowers tumbling from huge terracotta urns. Inside, nothing is spared in recreating a rich yet unstuffy grandeur. The overall effect is seductive and luminous: no wonder it's adored by the belligenti. When the summer air hums with cicadas, a small high-walled pool acts as a natural social hub.

C'est si bon!

Fantasy brought beautifully to life in a Florentine style villa.

Bon repos This is the place to slumber in a four-poster suite complete with plump bed, designer fabrics, thoughtful touches and a private terrace made for petit déjeuner al fresco. Tuck into flakiest croissants, piping hot coffee and marzipan calisson cakes in the heady morning air.

Bon appetit Sunshine flirts through shady trees on to the main terrace, while lavender scents the candlelight at dusk. Chef Christophe Gavot's inspired menu du terroir, with appropriate wines, majors on provençal specialities using tip-top ingredients, dense flavours and herbal nuances.

Bon temps Aix, at the base of Montagne St. Victoire, is quintessentially French. Baroque architecture, winding streets, old churches, gurgling fountains and blue-green trees are lit by the soft sunlight and warm colours that inspired Cézanne and the Impressionists. Visit his atelier, scour markets, museums and antique shops and check out the many festivals.

Bon voyage Follow the yellow signs from the city centre.

The Pyrenees

The Pyrenees:
From Pau to Perpignan

Aller for mountain highs
Manger cassoulet, poule au pot, confit de canard
Santé! Local Muscat, Côtes de Roussillon

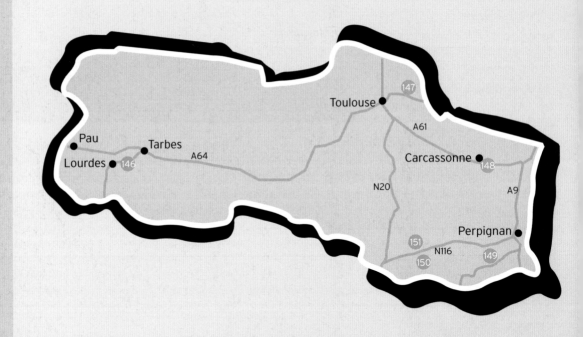

Roads ————

Pages 146 – 151

Why?

Green and rolling in the West, and rising to dramatic peaks further East, the Pyrenees form a jagged backdrop to France's southern borders. Waterfalls and forests spill down into verdant valleys, orchards and sun-bleached villages, where sheep-grazed slopes fringe whitewashed shuttered houses. Come here for winter skiing, summer walking and fabulously healthy fresh air - not to mention the colourful shades of Catalonia.

So why not...♥

- See nature at its wildest in the Parc National des Pyrénées
- Lace up your boots and head for the hills:
  walking trails are everywhere
- Feeling lazy? Stay in the saddle and go donkey trekking
- Stroll past Pau's galleried Béarnaise houses and
  palm-lined boulevards
- Check out the weird and wonderful works of Salvador Dali
  in Perpignan

Le Relais de Saux

Route de Tarbes, Le Hameau
de Saux, 65100 Lourdes
Tel: +33 (0) 5 62 94 29 61
Fax: +33 (0) 5 62 42 12 64
contact@lourdes-relais.com
www.lourdes-relais.com

Rooms and rates
6 rooms
Double room for 2 people
per night from €84 to €96
Breakfast €9. Dinner from €28

Proprietors
Madeleine and Bernard Hères

Open
All year round

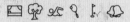

Fling the white shutters wide against the ivy-covered walls and soak up the view across the flowering terraces and emerald lawns to the jagged peaks of the Pyrenees. Bernard and Madeleine Hères are delightful, highly knowledgeable people with an eye for detail and a fund of stories who have turned this centuries-old fortified house (you can still see the old arrow slits in the walls) into a dreamy country retreat on a hillside facing the pilgrim town of Lourdes. As Bernard is fond of saying, you can practice all manner of playful activities here and still be close enough to Lourdes for some repentance afterwards!

C'est si bon!

A place to play, sin and (possibly) repent a stone's throw from Lourdes.

Bon repos Luscious bedrooms with huge picture windows on the first floor make the most of streaming sunshine and spectacular views. Cosier quarters on the upper floor are designed with comfort in mind. All have antique furniture and palatial beds, while one room has a fine old fireplace.

Bon appetit Forget any good intentions: the chef scours local markets to take you on an authentic gastronomic tour of south-west France. Dinner in the heavy-beamed dining room with its Spanish-style stone hearth is a feast for the senses with foie gras, lobster and bitter chocolate truffles star-studding a lavish menu.

Bon temps Prepare to embrace the great outdoors, with golf, fishing and mountain walking in summer or skiing in winter. There are castles, monasteries and museums in the town and surrounds, and a visit to the Donjon des Aigles, with its spectacular birds of prey displays, is a must.

Bon voyage From Toulouse: take A64, exit 12, to Tarbes and N21 towards Lourdes. The hamlet of Saux is just past Adé.

Cuq en Terrasses

Cuq-le-Château
81470 Cuq Toulza
Tel: +33 (0) 5 63 82 54 00
Fax: +33 (0) 5 63 82 54 11
info@cuqenterrasses.com
www.cuqenterrasses.com

Rooms and rates
8 rooms
Double room for 2 people
per night from €90 to €130
Breakfast €11. Dinner €30

Proprietor
Philippe Gallice

Open
April - October

Perched on a rocky slope in the centre of a triangle formed by Toulouse, Carcassonne and Albi, this four-storey stone house with its painted shutters exudes an air of warmth and comfort. The garden is a blaze of colour, and there's an inviting pool for days when you need to beat the heat. Nooks and crannies abound. Hand-finished plastered walls and terracotta-tiled floors are set off by glazed ceramics, woven rugs, crisp cottons, antique beds and varnished wood. There's a hillside terrace perfect for evening aperitifs, while the poolside suite (a former dovecote) makes a ravishing lovers' retreat perfect for midnight dips. Bliss!

C'est si bon!

Decadent living and midnight dips... a real mountain high.

Bon repos Antiques, original art, beams and individual decor lend the rooms warmth and character The troglodyte-style Terrace room has its own Roman shower, while the Terracotta room is filled with provençal art and sculpture. Expect robes and fluffy towels, with candles and aromatic bath essences on call for the ultimate soak.

Bon appetit Feast overlooking sunflower fields on produce fresh from local markets. Cooking here has a Mediterranean touch: dine on veal tagine or quail fillets with a honey and cranberry sauce, rounded off, perhaps, with a wicked strawberry and white chocolate cheesecake.

Bon temps Local markets offer scope for endless browsing. Walks start from the front door, and tennis, gliding, horse riding, mountain biking and windsurfing can all be arranged nearby. Carcassonne, Albi and vibrant Toulouse, with its big-city attractions, are a short drive away.

Bon voyage From Toulouse: take the N126 to Cuq Toulza, then D45 towards Revel.

Château de Floure

1 allée Gaston Bonheur
11800 Floure
Tel: +33 (0) 4 68 79 11 29
Fax: +33 (0) 4 68 79 04 61
contact@chateau-de-floure.com
www.chateau-de-floure.com

Rooms and rates
10 rooms, 3 apartments, 3 suites
Double room for 2 people
per night from €100 to €130
Breakfast from €16. Dinner from €39

Proprietors
Dominique and Jerry Assous

Open
Mid March – early January

The pleasing symmetry of this handsomely proportioned ivy-clad building, with its giant plane trees and perfectly balanced parterres curved into swirling shapes, arrests the eye. Completing this pretty scene are rose bushes, an old vineyard, a sun-facing terrace, conservatory and pool. Once a Roman villa, and now flanked by cottages and outbuildings, Château de Floure has a rich and interesting history. The main salon is decked with 18th century paintings, while elegant fauteuils add grace and charm. There's a friendly and caring atmosphere, not least because owners Jerry and Dominique Assous lead from the front.

C'est si bon!

Pastoral delights just
ten minutes from
Carcassonne.

Bon repos Gaze from some windows and the verdigris outline of Mount Alaric gazes back (sigh!). Rooms are spaciously proportioned and agreeably done up: you could find yourself snuggling down in a magnificently embroidered half-tester bed.

Bon appetit The restaurant is intriguingly called Le Poète Disparu. But good cooking certainly isn't missing: lip-smacking cuisine du terroir might include confit of duck, cassoulet, game and red mullet. Don't overlook drinks in the bar beforehand, or quaffable Aude wine with meals. There's a sheltered courtyard for summer dining.

Bon temps Get your fill of castles, abbeys, gorges, canals and lakes. Nearby Carcassonne, a World Heritage site walled city, is a medieval corker. Check out 13th century Fontfroide, founded by the Cistercians, and a wealth of museums. Or simply enjoy the hotel's pool and tennis court.

Bon voyage From Toulouse: take the A61 and join N113 at Carcassonne Est. The village of Floure is after Trèbes.

Le Mas Trilles

Le Pont de Reynès
66400 Céret
Tel: +33 (0) 4 68 87 38 37
Fax: +33 (0) 4 68 87 42 62
le-mas-trilles@romantikhotels.com
www.romantikhotels.com/ceret

Rooms and rates
9 rooms, 1 suite
Double room for 2 people
per night from €90 to €216
Breakfast included

Proprietor
Laszlo and Marie-France Bukk

Open
9 April - 7 October

Three 17th century golden-stone buildings make up this welcoming little hotel sitting snugly amid wooded hills and overlooking a river not far from the Spanish border. A rustic Catalan feel pervades the place, with cool tiled floors, plants trailing from terracotta pots and the scent of lavender and rosemary drifting in from nearby fields. Interiors are a pleasing blend of old and new. There's a garden filled with flowering shrubs and plenty of shady corners in which to relax, with little but the chorus of cicadas to disturb your peace. Owners Laszlo and Marie-France Bukk have created a warm, informal atmosphere in this unspoiled setting.

C'est si bon!

Shades of España in this relaxed little place near the Spanish border.

Bon repos Immaculate bedrooms are clutter-free and designed to stay cool on warm days, with tiled floors, light neutral shades and plenty of space. Almost all have either a terrace or small private garden for afternoon siestas.

Bon appetit This is a place to enjoy breakfast in the sunshine with crusty fresh brioches and plates of fresh fruit. Staff are happy to rustle up nibbles or a light lunch later, and your hosts will be delighted to suggest good dining-out spots in the locality.

Bon temps While you may be tempted to lounge around the pool, there's no shortage of scenic walks here. The gated town of Céret is close by, with its cherry trees, narrow streets, lively Saturday market and excellent modern art museum complete with Picasso and Chagall originals. The pretty hillside spa town of Amélie-les-Bains is a short drive in the other direction.

Bon voyage From Perpignan: take N9 south, then the D115 to Céret. Continue for 2km towards Amélie-les-Bains.

Les Ecureuils

66340 Valcebollere
Cerdagne
Tel: +33 (0) 4 68 04 52 03
Fax: +33 (0) 4 68 04 52 34
auberge-ecureuils@wanadoo.fr
www.paisos-catalans.com

Rooms and rates
15 rooms
Double room for 2 people
per night from €70 to €103
Breakfast from €9. Dinner from €25

Proprietors
Etienne and Patricia Lafitte

Open
All year except 1-21 May

You'll be as bright eyed as the squirrels this mountain auberge is named after following a few days' R&R at Les Ecureuils, in the heart of the French Pyrenees. This former 18th century farmhouse looks across the sunny Cerdagne valley – robed in snow in winter, jewelled in mountain streams in spring, and rich in flowers and birdlife – where the air is fresh enough to bottle. Run by Patricia and Etienne Lafitte (he acts as trail guide by day and chef by night), the inn is as appealing inside as out, with all the character and cosiness you'd expect. Outside, all is peace in this little Eden.

C'est si bon!

Snug Pyrenean hideaway on the French frontiers.

Bon repos Squirrel under the sheets in inviting bedrooms whose rafters and fine oak fittings radiate warmth. One has a king-size four-poster (worth splashing out for), while bathrooms are all tiled in Spanish marble. Needless to say, most offer terrific valley views.

Bon appetit Dining is a highlight here. There's a touch of ecclesiastical finery about the restaurant, with its stained glass windows, tall candelabra, open hearth and exposed stone walls. Tuck into hearty Catalan cooking whose ingredients reflect the seasons and locality. Nibble on tapas or delicious crêpes if you're not up to the full works.

Bon temps Mountains are the big attraction here – for walking, riding, skiing and fishing. There's a fitness room and sauna on site, as well as a book-lined salon to curl up in. You're close enough to Spain to pop over for coffee, while still feeling you're in a glorious outpost of La France.

Bon voyage From Perpignan: take the N116, turning left after Saillagouse on to the D30. Continue through Osséja.

L'Auberge Atalaya

66800 Llo
Pyrénées-Orientales
Tel: +33 (0) 4 68 04 70 04
Fax: +33 (0) 4 68 04 01 29
atalaya66@aol.com
(website under construction)

Rooms and rates
13 rooms, I suite
Double room for 2 people
per night from €90 to €140
Breakfast €11. Dinner from €30

Proprietor
Ghilaine Toussaint

Open
Easter - 20 January (not November)

High in the Cerdagne region - a place of plunging gorges, tumbling streams and green meadows - this ravishing Catalan farmhouse sits pretty in a village complete with ruined castle and watchtower just a whisker from the Spanish border. Nature lovers will have a field day in this heady domain, famed for its butterflies, wild flowers and birdlife. Encircled by snowy peaks in winter and sheep-grazed slopes in summer, Atalaya is quite simply a treat. Vine-covered walls lead the way to inviting rooms furnished with antiques, a grand piano and a terrace with views too good to be true.

C'est si bon!

Peace and poetic views in a ravishing Pyrenean hideaway.

Bon repos Artistic owner Ghilaine Toussaint has lavished care and attention on her guests' quarters. Bedrooms (all different) are done out in the glowing colours of the South - peach, cream and sienna - with fine fabrics and original art. Some have canopied beds and their own private terrace.

Bon appetit Gaze out on Spanish hills as you breakfast on fresh croissants, juices and steaming coffee on the terrace. Dinner is a similar treat in the lamplit dining room, with its rustic stone walls, fresh flowers and crisp linen tablecloths. Regional cuisine is generously, and elegantly, served here.

Bon temps Head for the pool terrace for refreshing dips and lazy afternoon siestas. Check out the area's markets, museums and baroque churches, or the hot springs in the village. Pop to Andorra for lunch, take mountain walks, ride horseback, make it love-all at tennis or hone your handicap on scenic fairways.

Bon voyage From Perpignan: take the N116 to Saillagouse, then join the D33 to Llo and Eyne.

Index by hotels

Certain hotel affiliations are also shown below

Index by place name

 ● Les Hôtels Particuliers Groupe Savry

 ● Relais & Châteaux

 ● Rocco Forte Hotels

 ● Baglioni Hotels

 ● Groupe Lucien Barrière

 ● Sofitel

Room for Romance

www.room4romance.com

Do visit Room for Romance online. You'll find a regularly updated bulletin board detailing news and special offers at our hotels, together with interactive maps and a picture of each property. There are direct links to each of the 120 places to stay featured in this guide - plus another 90 selected hotels in the UK and Ireland - making it the simplest way to check availability at any Room for Romance property. You can also see what the press say about us, email your comments and feedback, and see details of the Room for Romance Hotels of the Year.

Room for Romance - Great Britain and Ireland

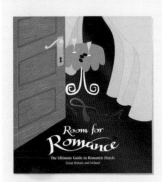

If Room for Romance - France has inspired you to take off on a romantic break, you need a copy of our sister edition covering Great Britain and Ireland. Tailor-made for lovers of good hotels, it's packed with details of places to fall in love with - and in love in.

The 120-page guide features 90 properties ranging from grand country manors to cosy inns and plum designer addresses. There are places perfect for playing Lord and Lady of the Manor, chic city bolt-holes and intimate hideaways where sweethearts won't want to surface. You'll find properties located everywhere from London to the west of Ireland - many boasting lovers' must-haves like four-poster beds, jacuzzis made for two, double hammocks and individually themed bedrooms.

To order a copy, call 020 7739 1434 or visit www.room4romance.com

Getting to France

Getting to France by air has never been easier. The growth of low-cost airline services and low fares in recent years means you can often fly direct to the region or city you want, at a bargain price. While routes and operators can change at short notice, the following list is correct at the time of going to press. Book on the web for the best fares.

BERGERAC
Bristol - FlyBE; **Southampton** - FlyBE; **Stansted** - Ryanair

BIARRITZ
Stansted - Ryanair

BORDEAUX
Birmingham - British Airways; **Bristol** - FlyBE; **Gatwick** - Air France, British Airways, FlyBE

BREST
Stansted - Ryanair

CARCASSONNE
Stansted - Ryanair

DINARD
Stansted - Ryanair

LA ROCHELLE
Southampton - FlyBE; **Stansted** - Ryanair

LIMOGES
Southampton - FlyBE; **Stansted** - Ryanair

LYON
London Heathrow - British Airways; **Manchester** - British Airways; **Stansted** - Easyjet

MARSEILLE
Gatwick - British Airways, Easyjet

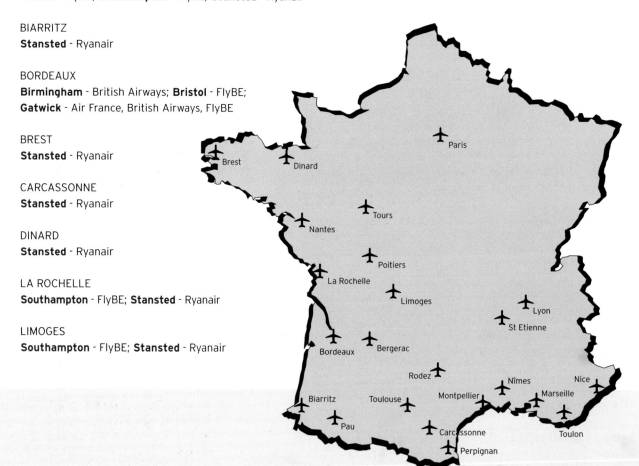

MONTPELLIER
Gatwick - British Airways; **Stansted** - Ryanair

NANTES
Gatwick - British Airways, FlyBE

NICE
Bristol - Easyjet; **Gatwick** - British Airways, Easyjet; **Liverpool** - Easyjet; **London Heathrow** - Air France, British Airways, British Midland; **Luton** - Easyjet; **Manchester** - British Airways; **East Midlands** - Bmibaby; **Stansted** - Easyjet; **Teeside** - BMIbaby

NîMES
Stansted - Ryanair

PARIS
Aberdeen - Air France, FlyBE; **Belfast** - British Airways; **Birmingham** - Air France, British Airways; **Bristol** - Air France, British Airways, FlyBE; **Cardiff** - Bmibaby; **Edinburgh** - Air France, British Airways, FlyBE; **Gatwick** - British Airways; **Glasgow** - British Airways; **Leeds-Bradford** - British Midland; **Liverpool** - Easyjet; **London City** - FlyBE; **London Heathrow** - Air France, British Airways, British Midland, FlyBE; **Luton** - Easyjet; **Manchester** - Air France, British Airways, FlyBE; **Newcastle** - Air France, Easyjet; **East Midlands** - BMIbaby; **Southampton** - Air France, FlyBE

PAU
Stansted - Ryanair

PERPIGNAN
Stansted - Ryanair

POITIERS
Stansted - Ryanair

RODEZ
Stansted - Ryanair

ST-ETIENNE
Stansted - Ryanair
TOULON
Gatwick - British Airways

TOULOUSE
Aberdeen - British Midland; **Birmingham** - FlyBE; **Bristol** - FlyBE; **Cardiff** - BMIbaby; **Edinburgh** - British Midland; **Gatwick** - British Airways, Easyjet; **Glasgow** - British Midland; **Manchester** - British Midland; **East Midlands** - BMIbaby; **Southampton** - FlyBE

TOURS
Stansted - Ryanair

For details of rail and ferry operators, see page 158.

Contact details

Air France 0845 359 1000
www.airfrance.com/uk
BMIbaby 0870 264 2229
www.bmibaby.com
British Airways 0870 850 9850
www.ba.com

British Midland 0870 6070 555
www.flybmi.com
Easyjet 08717 500 100
www.easyjet.com
FlyBE 08717 000 353
www.flybe.com

Monarch Scheduled 0870 0405 040
www.flymonarch.com
MyTravelLite 0870 1564 564
www.mytravellite.com
Ryanair 0871 2460 000
www.ryanair.com

Useful contacts

CAR HIRE COMPANIES

Alamo
0870 400 4562
www.alamo.co.uk

Avis
08700 100 287
www.avis.co.uk

Budget
0870 153 9170
www.budget.co.uk

EasyCar
0906 333 3333
www.easycar.com

Europcar
0870 607 5000
www.europcar.co.uk

Hertz
08708 448 844
www.hertz.co.uk

Holiday Autos
0870 400 4447
www.holidayautos.co.uk

National
0870 400 4581
www.nationalcar.co.uk

RAIL AND CHANNEL TUNNEL

Eurostar
08705 186 186
www.eurostar.com
London Waterloo to Paris, Lille, Disneyland Paris and Avignon

Le Shuttle
08705 353 535
www.eurotunnel.com

CROSS-CHANNEL FERRIES

Brittany Ferries
0870 366 5333
www.brittanyferries.com
Portsmouth to Caen, Saint Malo and Cherbourg. Poole to Cherbourg. Plymouth to Roscoff

Condor Ferries
0845 345 2000
www.condorferries.com
Poole to Saint Malo and Cherbourg. Portsmouth to Cherbourg. Weymouth to Saint Malo.

Hoverspeed
0870 240 8070
www.hoverspeed.com
Dover to Calais. Newhaven to Dieppe.

P & O Ferries
08705 202 020
www.poferries.com
Dover to Calais. Portsmouth to Le Havre and Cherbourg.

Seafrance
0870 443 1685
www.seafrance.com
Dover to Calais.

FRENCH TOURIST BOARD

London
Maison de la France
178 Piccadilly
London W1J 9AL
09068 244 123
www.franceguide.com

Paris
+33 (0) 1 42 96 70 00

www.tourisme.fr (for regional tourist offices)

How was it for you?

Much as we have enjoyed selecting the places to stay featured within these pages, no guide is perfect. Owners change, chefs move on and excellent properties can lose their touch. Your experiences and views count, and we value your feedback when it comes to ensuring that our chosen properties live up to the standards that you – and we – expect.

So please share your views with us. Tell us which places you liked, and why – or if any fell short of your expectations. We'd also like to hear about your own discoveries; little gems or grand estates which you think should be included in a future edition of Room for Romance – France. Our team will be pleased to receive, and check out, your personal recommendations.

Vote for the ultimate Room for Romance

Which of the wonderful places featured among these pages is the ultimate romantic place to stay in France? Here's your chance to see that your views count when we hand out bouquets. The Room for Romance Hotel of the Year awards are announced on 1 February, and you'll see the winners' names published on our website, and in the press. Awards are based on what you, our readers, tell us.*

Tell us about any memorable occasions you spent at a Room for Romance hotel in France. We have a magnum of superb Perrier-Jouët champagne to give away to the person who sends us the best, most original or entertaining letter in the run-up to our awards. Look out, too, for competitions in the press where you may have the opportunity to win a stay at a Room for Romance award-winning hotel.

* Votes from family, friends or employees of any featured property are, needless to say, ineligible.

TO CONTACT US
Write to:
The Editor, Room for Romance, 4 Ravey Street, London EC2A 4XX
info@room4romance.com

Le Moulin de Crouy
Tel 02 54 87 56 19
3 Route de la Pondellerie
Crouy-sur-Cosson.
65/67 Eur
Repas 25 E

Parlez-vous...?

Whether you're away celebrating l'amour fou (wild passion), a grand amour (the big one), or merely an amourette (a delightful fling), you may like to know how to order some of these romantic essentials – or explain why it's a special occasion – to make the most of your stay.

Could we have...?	**Serait-il possible d'avoir...?**
Bathrobes	**Peignoirs**
Bowl of strawberries	**Une coupe de fraises**
Breakfast in bed	**Petit déjeuner au lit/dans la chambre**
Bubble bath	**Bain mousseux**
Caviar, lobster	**Caviar, homard**
Champagne on ice	**Une bouteille de champagne en seau**
Do not disturb	**Ne pas déranger**
Double/king size bed	**Un 'king-size'**
Extra pillows	**Oreillers supplémentaires**
Flowers and chocolates	**Des fleurs et chocolats**
Four poster/canopied bed	**Un lit baldaquin**
Ice bucket	**Un seau**
It's a special occasion	**C'est pour un événement**
It's our anniversary/honeymoon/wedding night	**C'est notre anniversaire/voyage de noces/ jour de mariage**
Overnight room service	**Service d'étage pendant la nuit**
No calls, please	**Pas d'appels, s'il vous plaît**
Sparkling wine	**Vin mousseux**
Red roses	**Roses rouges**
We're celebrating	**Nous fêtons...**
We've just got engaged/married	**Nous venons de nous fiancer/marier**
Whirlpool bath	**Bain à remous**

Room for Romance

Freeway Media Ltd, 4 Ravey Street, London EC2A 4XX
T +44 (0)20 7739 1434   **F** +44 (0)20 7739 1424
info@room4romance.com   www.room4romance.com